The A–Z
Guide to Exposure

THE A–Z GUIDE TO EXPOSURE

Creative ERP Activities for 75 Childhood Fears

Dawn Huebner, PhD
Erin Neely, PsyD

Jessica Kingsley Publishers
London and Philadelphia

First published in Great Britain in 2023 by Jessica Kingsley Publishers
An imprint of Hodder & Stoughton Ltd
An Hachette Company

2

Copyright © Dawn Huebner and Erin Neely 2023

The right of Dawn Huebner and Erin Neely to be identified as
the Author of the Work has been asserted by them in accordance
with the Copyright, Designs and Patents Act 1988.

A CIP catalogue record for this title is available from the
British Library and the Library of Congress

ISBN 978 1 83997 322 2
eISBN 978 1 83997 323 9

Printed and bound in Great Britain by CPI Group (UK) Ltd, Croydon CR0 4YY

Jessica Kingsley Publishers' policy is to use papers that are natural,
renewable, and recyclable products and made from wood grown in
sustainable forests. The logging and manufacturing processes are expected
to conform to the environmental regulations of the country of origin.

Jessica Kingsley Publishers
Carmelite House
50 Victoria Embankment
London EC4Y 0DZ

www.jkp.com

Contents

Introduction

The A–Z Guide to Exposure contains 75 creative, user-friendly lists of exposure activities appropriate for 5–12-year-olds who struggle with anxiety.

WHY DID WE WRITE THIS BOOK?

Erin: I co-wrote this book because I needed it! Until now, whenever I worked with a child who needed Exposure and Response Prevention (ERP), I had to write a new exposure list from scratch or go digging around in past clients' charts to find an old list to work from. No matter how hard I looked, I could not find a book about exposure that met my needs as a therapist.

I found plenty of books thick with theory, extolling the virtues of Exposure and Response Prevention. But I was already sold, I knew I needed to do exposure with my child clients. What I really needed was a simple guide that allowed me to flip to the relevant page and get a well-thought-out list of creative, child-friendly activities. So, that's the book we wrote. Even while working on it, I was using this book almost daily.

Dawn: I remember studying exposure decades ago. When a child is afraid of heights, I learned, you take them to high places. When a child is afraid of vomiting, you make them throw up. I was a graduate student at the time, and I remember thinking, "Wait! What? How can making a child throw up possibly be the answer?"

It turns out, it isn't. Exposure isn't a fill-in-the-blank enterprise. In the case of emetophobia, what you induce is apprehension. You expose the child to the people, places, clothing, and foods they associate with throwing up. Inducing vomit doesn't figure in.

There is an art to exposure, and plenty of hard work that goes into crafting targeted, perfectly pitched challenges. Get the challenges wrong and the technique is doomed to fail. Get them right and you set the child free. The power and beauty of exposure is the reason I said yes to Erin when she asked me to co-write this book.

WHO IS THIS BOOK FOR?

This book is for you, therapists and counselors who understand the basics of Cognitive Behavior Therapy (CBT) and have experience treating childhood anxiety. It is also for graduate students learning about ERP, and parents working with a cognitive-behaviorally oriented therapist.

WHAT WILL NOT BE COVERED IN THIS BOOK?

This book is not a comprehensive treatment manual. It does not go into detail about theory, nor does it cover the extensive research supporting Exposure and Response Prevention as a treatment method. Therapists retain responsibility for the decisions they make when using these lists, keeping in mind that exposure is a single tool in what is hopefully a hefty therapeutic toolbox.

WHAT IS EXPOSURE AND RESPONSE PREVENTION (ERP)?

ERP is a cognitive behavioral treatment method. Research has repeatedly and consistently supported its efficacy in the treatment of anxiety, phobias, and Obsessive Compulsive Disorder (OCD). The decision to use exposure is guided by the Jungian maxim: What we resist, persists. Anything a child is resisting, running away from, stymied by, or stuck on can be treated with ERP.

Exposure refers to the intentional practice of facing what is causing anxiety. Response prevention refers to resisting the natural urge to reduce anxiety. So, for example, when doing ERP to treat anxiety about dogs, you would expose the child to a dog while preventing them from running away.

WHAT ARE SAFETY BEHAVIORS?

Safety behaviors are behaviors a child engages in to protect themself from imagined danger. In the example above, running away would be considered a safety behavior. Anxious children reach for safety behaviors to keep their uncertainty, discomfort, and fear at bay. Things like checking, reassurance-seeking, avoiding, undoing, re-doing, confessing, mental rituals, insistence on sameness, and constant distraction are all safety behaviors. When a child completes a safety behavior, they feel better. And often the perceived danger doesn't come to pass, which children mistakenly attribute to having done their safety behavior.

It's easy to fall into the habit of using safety behaviors for the relief they bring and the protective value they appear to hold. But there's a catch. It's not the safety behavior that keeps the child safe; they are already safe. Because safety behaviors create the illusion of safety and bring relief, they end up reinforcing unproductive responses to anxiety, which is why response prevention is an essential part of ERP.

HOW DOES ERP WORK?

Exposure works through the process of habituation. When we are exposed to the same thing repeatedly or for a long time, we get used to it and have less of an emotional reaction to it. It's like wearing pants; we are so accustomed to wearing them that, at any given moment, we don't notice we have them on.

ERP focuses on feared targets and safety behaviors. Because safety behaviors create the illusion of safety, when you prevent the child from performing them, anxiety increases. So, every time you expose a child to a feared target and prevent them from doing their safety behaviors, you are also exposing them to the experience of anxiety. By intentionally facing imagined dangers without safety behaviors, the child develops tolerance for their anxiety and learns that the feared thing is not likely to happen. As such, ERP retrains the brain, teaching it to more accurately distinguish between actual dangers and false alarms.

Exposure and Response Prevention progresses sequentially, starting with the least feared and moving toward the most feared scenario. For example, a child with a bird phobia might start with writing the word *bird* and work toward visiting a bird sanctuary.

Exposure occurs frequently. Depending on the circumstance, exposure could happen as often as several times a day. The child with the bird phobia might have a cuddly bird toy in their bed, go on a bird scavenger hunt on their way home from school, and make a bird craft after dinner.

Exposures are intentional, such as in a planned hierarchy, as well as naturally occurring. For example, the plan might include how to respond to birds the child serendipitously encounters on their way to the bus. Whether naturally occurring or choreographed, exposure is something we want the child to be aware of, and to do on purpose.

> **Three Kinds of Exposure**
>
> ✓ In vivo: direct challenges involving real-life contact with the feared situations
>
> ✓ In vitro: imaginal challenges in which the child pictures the feared situation
>
> ✓ Virtual: challenges that use technology to simulate the feared situation

Finally, well-crafted ERP plans incorporate the child's and family's interests and values. Children's lives become restricted by their fears. The therapist is well positioned to champion the message that when these fears are addressed, the child's world will open significantly and they will be free to do the things they want and deserve to do. The child with the bird fear, for example, might be at risk of missing out on a ferry ride the family has planned. The therapist can talk about how fun it will be to take the ride together, and incorporate exposures to seagulls to help make the trip possible. In this way, individualized interventions are not only ethical practice, they also boost the effectiveness of treatment.

WHAT TECHNIQUES SUPPLEMENT THE USE OF EXPOSURE?

Exposure is typically done as part of a cognitive-behaviorally oriented therapy. Other cognitive techniques, including labeling anxiety, hypothesis testing, self-talk, and evaluating likelihood, all enrich exposure.

Children with anxiety often require support for self-regulation. As such, the therapist will also likely teach breathing techniques, mindfulness strategies, and positive distraction. An important caveat: self-regulation strategies are meant to support children in daily life, and they typically reduce reactivity. They are not, however, meant to be used during exposure as it is necessary for children to experience their fear. That's how cognitive restructuring takes place.

Keep in mind that exposure works best when there is a strong, positive relationship between the therapist and child. For this reason, therapeutic play, active listening, empathic reflection, and co-regulation are often part of the therapeutic plan.

Helpful Self-Talk

"Being anxious is hard. Doing exposure is hard. I choose the hard that makes my life better."

"There is nothing dangerous here. This is just anxiety."

"I've handled harder things than this."

"I will feel so much better when this is done."

"I can see this through."

"I am strong."

"It's just worry. I don't have to listen."

"Worry is not the boss of me."

"I am brave."

"What I'm feeling is a false alarm."

HOW DO YOU KNOW IF A CHILD IS READY FOR ERP?

Readiness to start ERP begins with age-appropriate psychoeducation about the purpose of anxiety and how it interacts with the brain and body. We teach children and parents that we are primed to protect ourselves from things that might hurt us. When we encounter something new, or when we feel unsure about a situation, our brain sets off an alarm. This alarm, which we experience as anxiety, is a normal, healthy response to possible danger. Our brains err on the side of over-protecting, which means we end up having "false alarms" when anxiety is triggered even though we are safe.

There are several ways to teach our brains to distinguish between real dangers and false alarms. One is to question, and ultimately disobey, anxiety. In other words, we expose ourselves to the things we fear rather than backing away from them. If we don't do what anxiety is telling us and nothing bad happens, we learn we are safe. Repeating this again and again cements the lesson, quieting anxiety and rewiring the brain. When children understand this process, they understand the basics of ERP.

In addition to understanding anxiety, it is also important for the therapeutic relationship to be in place before starting ERP. It is best to do exposure *with* the child, not *to* the child, which means that time must be taken to establish rapport and build trust.

The at-home portion of exposure is dependent on children feeling emotionally safe with their parents. Time is often devoted to coaching parents to use self-regulation strategies so they can co-regulate when the child gets anxious. It is essential for parents to know how to provide calm, steady support while doing exposures at home.

Before starting ERP, the therapist must determine that this is the right intervention for a particular child. The child's well-being must be stable enough to tolerate the stress of ERP, which may cause the therapist to turn to other interventions first.

WHAT ARE THE CONTRAINDICATIONS FOR EXPOSURE?

Exposure is a powerful, highly effective technique, but it isn't always the right technique. Before launching into exposure-based therapy, and assuming readiness has been assessed, it is important for therapists to ask themselves two additional questions: Under what circumstances would this symptom make sense? And why else might the child be having trouble? The two most common answers have to do with comorbidities and trauma.

Anxiety seldom occurs in isolation. Many children have "anxiety plus," with add-ons such as sensory differences, learning challenges, underlying medical diagnoses, food sensitivities, and additional psychiatric diagnoses. Sometimes exposure needs to be delayed while these concerns are stabilized. Sometimes ERP needs to be modified, for example using ear protection for a child with sensory sensitivities or allowing a limited amount of checking for a child with food allergies.

Therapists must also proceed with caution when a child has a history of trauma or is significantly stressed in some way, such as a child whose parents have just separated or a child living in an unsafe environment. The behaviors that arise under these circumstances are better treated with trauma-informed care prior to, and sometimes instead of, exposure-based therapy.

Additionally, the therapist should assess the parents' ability to regulate themselves. If the child's distress during exposure is likely to be significantly unsettling to a parent, exposure should be delayed. The therapist may need to provide coaching prior to initiating ERP, or the parent might benefit from therapy of their own.

HOW DO YOU GET STARTED WITH AN ERP PLAN?

Once you have established that ERP is the correct method of intervention, work with the child and parent to make a list of fears and corresponding safety behaviors. Decide together which fear to address first. Try to find something manageable that the child is motivated to work on, something that will improve the quality of life for everyone. Early success gives families the momentum needed to face harder challenges.

The next step is to make a list of exposure activities. Using *The A–Z Guide* for inspiration, work with the child and parent to create a customized list. Be both creative and specific as you think about ways to have the child practice facing the target fear. Include challenges that are close to what the child is already capable of, challenges that seem far out of reach, and everything in between. Have the child organize the challenges into mildly, moderately, and significantly anxiety provoking. Start with a challenge the child and parent see as relatively easy and do-able over the course of the next week.

Exposure therapy rests firmly on the trust and mutual regard the therapist has built. This includes convincing the child that the therapist does not want to be *yes*-ed. The child should only agree to challenges they are willing to do. If a challenge seems too hard, we want the child to say so in the session, not after. This should be talked about explicitly, underlining that the child, parent, and therapist are full partners in the work of exposure.

Finding Content

1. Always search ahead of time and properly vet content before showing or recommending.

2. Start on a general search engine. Click video and image tabs for more ideas. You are likely to see books, videos, images, games, and more.

3. Move to content-specific search engines: YouTube and TikTok for videos, app stores for apps and games.

4. Search terms are key. Start with broad terms such as *vomit* or *boats* before moving to more specific terms like *vomit illustration* or *view from boat*. Try synonyms like *barf* or *throw up* or less specific terms, such as *sick* or *illness*.

5. Be on the lookout for material related to common fears. If you see a good book about spiders, buy it. If you see a game about bees, download it.

6. Parents often want to know how they can help. Assisting in the search is something pragmatic they can do.

HOW CHALLENGING SHOULD EXPOSURES BE?

Aim for a "just-right" level of difficulty, neither too easy nor too hard. That being said, at the start of treatment the child may only feel up to doing the easiest of challenges. That's okay. Keep in mind that the child is gauging how well they can trust the process and whether they can handle it. Once they have a few successes under their belts, children often pick more challenging tasks.

HOW DO YOU EXPLAIN EXPOSURE
TO A CHILD AND THEIR PARENTS?

It is not uncommon for parents to feel frustrated by the small steps a child must take at the beginning of ERP. For a parent struggling with all-out battles about walking to the bus because their child is afraid of bees, it can be difficult to see how drawing pictures of bees is going to get them to school on time. Metaphors provide the framework for understanding the nature of ERP.

To address parental frustration, the therapist might begin with a marathon metaphor. When you decide to run a marathon, you don't just put on your shoes and run a marathon. You start by running a mile. If running a mile is too hard, you run down the street, or around the block. Or you walk. You find the right size step, and you do it. And then you do the next step. Each challenge, however small, moves you toward the larger goal.

A swimming pool metaphor, on the other hand, is easily relatable to children. When you initially get into a pool, the water feels cold. But you don't scramble out; you stay in and get used to the water. Similarly, with fears, we are going to find the right-size steps to help you "stay in" and get used to dealing with scary situations in a different way.

Another metaphor that resonates with children is chewing gum, as described in *What to Do When You Dread Your Bed*.[1] When you first put a piece of gum into your mouth, it has lots of flavor. As you chew and chew, the flavor goes away. Fear works like the flavor. As you do your challenges, you will be chewing away your fear.

WHAT IF THINGS DON'T GO AS EXPECTED?

There are a variety of hiccups common in ERP. Here's how to understand and manage them.

---

1   Huebner, D. (2008) *What to Do When You Dread Your Bed*. Washington, DC: Magination Press.

The child's anxiety appears worse. There is a phenomenon called an extinction burst, which happens when a child unconsciously tests the system to see if the parent is serious about this new way of doing things, and if they are strong enough to contain the child's big feelings. This is not something the child does on purpose; they are neither manipulating nor faking how they feel.

When a child is experiencing intense anxiety, if the parent gets flustered or angry, the child learns that their parent is unsettled by big feelings. Conversely, if the parent lets go of the exposure entirely, the child learns that they aren't going to be held accountable for doing hard things. Talking with parents about the extinction burst ahead of time makes it more likely they will work with the child to make the exposure a little smaller, which is exactly what we want them to do.

Exposure works best when the child consents to the plan and works cooperatively. That might mean temporarily moving back to an exposure the therapist knows is too easy. From there, the therapist can coordinate slow, steady progress by supporting the child to gradually tolerate more, consenting to the next challenge, and then the next. It won't be long before the child is able to trust the therapist, the process, and themself. Once this trust is in place, children are better able to pick the right level of challenge without their anxiety kicking up a fuss.

The child breezes through the challenge without a problem. Either the challenge was too easy or the therapist is approaching the fear from the wrong angle. Anxiety is fickle, attaching itself to some things and not others in a way that can seem illogical. A child might be anxious about saying a word, but not writing it. They might be anxious about seeing a parent do something that they are able to do themself. If a challenge was easier than expected, ask the child to think about why. Use that information to collaboratively choose the next challenge.

The child consents to a challenge, but when it comes time to do it, they want out. The solution to this problem is the same as for the extinction burst. Teach the parent to emotionally support the child as they work together to make the challenge a little smaller. Sticking doggedly to a planned exposure can escalate the child's emotions to an unhelpful level, rendering them unable to participate in their own treatment. Significant dysregulation is frightening for children. It undermines trust, and ultimately makes anxiety worse. It is better to slightly modify the challenge, to help the child see the process as do-able.

The family comes to the session having done the therapy homework in the car on the way over. This happens more often than you might think. Talk with the parent and child to understand what happened. Was the challenge not the right size? Did the child want out? Did other commitments get in the way? Help the family reconnect with why they signed up for this difficult process. What are they hoping therapy will do for them? How much time are they willing to spend on ERP? What are they looking forward to being able to do once the anxiety is quieter? Problem-solve about logistics and decide whether to repeat the same challenge or modify it in the coming week.

The family is unable to do their therapy homework. Be sure to normalize this while reminding the parent and child that at-home exposure is an essential part of therapy. Address misconceptions about exposure. Coach the parent to support the child without capitulating to their anxiety. Use the metaphors described earlier to explain the benefit of consistent, small steps. Collaborate to make the next challenge small enough to be do-able, as accomplishment creates the momentum for forward progress.

The parent is the one who breaks the agreement. This can go two ways. Sometimes in their eagerness to make progress, parents take things too far. They might, for example, think that if the child is successfully spending time alone, they should leave them in their room longer than the agreed upon time. In this scenario, the parent needs more information about the importance of trust, and how subtly extending exposures is likely to undermine the process.

It is never helpful to "pull one over" on a child when it comes to exposure. Children need to know what the challenge is and when it is happening. For example, when working on tolerating disruptions, the parent might say, "Now we're going to work on being interrupted. Let's start this game and when the timer goes off, we'll put the game away, no matter what is happening." The fact that an exposure is happening is always made clear.

Sometimes parents are ambivalent about exposing their child to anxiety. It's hard to see their child go through something difficult, and parents often feel compelled to reduce what they perceive as suffering. Parents prone to anxiety might have particular trouble tolerating their child's anxiety, stopping challenges prematurely or in other ways communicating that whatever the child is doing, or feeling, or facing is too hard.

It's important to talk about the downside of allowing anxiety to call the shots. Return to the basics of anxiety education, reminding the family that anxiety is there to protect us from danger but sometimes shows up at the wrong time, like when the child is safe. When you do what anxiety tells you to do, it gets bigger. When you don't do what anxiety says, it gets smaller. Taking the time to help parents and children understand ERP, and making sure they have the skills needed to tolerate the anxiety it triggers, helps families trust the process. You want them to see that the child's anxiety is uncomfortable but not dangerous, and that moving through the discomfort is do-able.

HOW DO YOU COACH FAMILIES TO MAKE DECISIONS ABOUT EXPOSURE?

It's best to be specific about exposure homework including what to do and how often to do it. At the same time, you want parents to understand how and under what circumstances to modify the plan. If you are using the pool analogy, talk about the importance of "staying in the water." If the child gets panicky, the goal is to take a single step back, not get out of the pool entirely.

Teach parents to creatively reduce the scariness of a challenge by altering a single feature. Maybe the child could close their eyes, or take one step away, or change the speed of what they are doing. Make sure the parent knows how to hold an encouraging stance. We don't want parents to do the equivalent of shoving the child into the water; there is no room for anger or punishment in healing.

It's important for parents to acknowledge that what is happening is hard, and to express faith in their child's ability to hang in there. Parents can say something along the lines of, "I can see that this feels hard. In a way, that's great because it means we picked the right size step. You're getting stronger every time." Warmth, encouragement, and gentle humor help children persevere.

There are different perspectives on how to move through an exposure hierarchy. Some therapists recommend doing an exposure a certain number of times before advancing to the next level. Others encourage families to wait for a check-in with the therapist before taking on new challenges. Either way, talk directly with the parent and child about how often you'd like them to practice, and for how long, and with which challenges, so there is a clear plan for what to do between therapy sessions.

IS THERE A PLACE FOR INCENTIVES AND REWARDS WITH EXPOSURE?

Absolutely. Incentives and rewards are positive reinforcement. Like the spoonful of sugar that helps the medicine go down, rewards make exposure more palatable for children, increasing the likelihood that a desired behavior will occur.

Keep in mind that crafting an effective reward system is a lot like baking. We need the right ingredients in the right proportion to one another. How hard are the challenges for this particular child? How long will they need to sustain effort? How well is this child able to tap into internal motivation and intrinsic pride? To what extent can they delay gratification? What kind of reward would be of interest to them? The answers to these questions determine the structure of the reward system.

Help parents avoid the temptation to offer grand enticements as these often turn out to be counterproductive. Since, for the most part, we are choosing challenges in the mild to moderately stressful range, incentives should be small to medium size. Keep in mind that it is typically more effective for this age group to offer relatively small rewards frequently than to expect them to put weeks of effort into earning something bigger. As children gain experience with exposure, you can expect more from the child and expand the interval between rewards.

Sample Reward List

- ✓ Double dessert
- ✓ Parent to do your chores for a day
- ✓ Family pillow fight
- ✓ Do a craft
- ✓ New item of clothing
- ✓ Eat watching a show
- ✓ Piggy-back ride to bed
- ✓ Trip to the library
- ✓ Stickers
- ✓ Collectibles
- ✓ Family game night
- ✓ Card tournament with parent
- ✓ Choose parent's clothes for the day
- ✓ Home spa (facials, nail polish)
- ✓ Go out for ice cream
- ✓ Extra snuggle time with parent
- ✓ Game with parent
- ✓ Extra book at bedtime
- ✓ New toy
- ✓ Family bike ride
- ✓ Treat in lunch box
- ✓ Parent to sing all requests for the morning
- ✓ Visit an animal shelter
- ✓ Stay up 15 minutes later
- ✓ Bowling
- ✓ Inside obstacle course
- ✓ Mystery outing
- ✓ Download a new app
- ✓ Backward dinner with dessert first
- ✓ Trip to the bookstore for a book
- ✓ Choose a treat at the grocery store
- ✓ Choose a family dinner
- ✓ Choose a family movie
- ✓ Camp out in the living room or outside
- ✓ Get 15 minutes extra screen time
- ✓ Build an indoor fort
- ✓ Build an outdoor fort
- ✓ Sleepover with a friend or relative
- ✓ Outing with parent
- ✓ No chores for a day
- ✓ Bake something
- ✓ Make ice cream sundaes
- ✓ Do a science experiment
- ✓ Get a new art supply
- ✓ Get video game currency
- ✓ Family picnic

It is often helpful to invite children to participate in choosing rewards, as incentives that hold no value to the child will be ineffective. On the other hand, some children enjoy the element of surprise, in which case a parent might put together a grab bag of perks and treats. Whether the parent is surprising the child or the child is choosing, rewards can take the form of an item, an experience, or a special privilege. Keep in mind that for many children, things that are motivating one week may not be the next, which means you cannot "set-and-forget" the reward system.

It is necessary for therapists to work with families to ensure that rewards are being used effectively. Monitoring the size and frequency of rewards is important, as is keeping tabs on everyone's understanding of what is being rewarded. Remember, it is cooperation with exposure that we are rewarding, not the absence of fear. You will also want to make sure the child is receiving what they have earned. In the busyness of daily life, it's easy for rewards to fall by the wayside, which is bad for morale.

Whether or not you are using a formal reward system, it is important to recognize children for the efforts they are making, and to teach parents to do the same. Be both genuine and generous with praise, pointing out how the child is benefiting from exposure. We want children to own what they are doing and feel good about their accomplishments as this supports the ever-important internal locus of control.

WHAT IS THE ROLE OF SAFETY IN ERP, ESPECIALLY WHEN A CHILD FEARS SOMETHING THAT IS TRULY DANGEROUS?

Exposure never puts a child in harm's way. This presents a puzzle when a child is afraid of something that is indeed dangerous. For example, some children have a crippling fear of bees, but it is good judgment to give bees a wide berth. So, we expose the child to being outdoors, where they *might* get stung. It's the possibility we are exposing the child to, not the actual bee sting. Another example: a child who fears that people who look at them might molest them would be exposed not to pedophiles but to public spaces where they are likely to be seen by strangers. And finally, a child who fears dying by suicide would be exposed to objects they are avoiding, like household knives.

There is often a kernel of truth embedded in fears; the feared outcome is possible, and it would be bad. Exposure aims to "rightsize" these fears, to help children see that possible is different from probable, and that thinking about something in no way makes it true.

Children should never be asked to do something the therapist wouldn't do. We strongly encourage you to try out unfamiliar exposures before assigning them. You might be surprised to find that breathing through a straw is more than a little alarming, and that watching videos of people vomiting can make you feel queasy yourself.

WHAT CAN GET IN THE WAY OF EFFECTIVE TREATMENT?

Insufficient preparation. Take the time to lay the groundwork for both the child and the parent. Exposure works best when everyone understands why it is being done. Be clear about what it means to "succeed" with an exposure.

Success is not the absence of fear. It is finding challenges that trigger mild to moderate fear, and doing them.

Choosing challenges that are too hard, especially early on. Children who make their way into therapy often have low distress tolerance. Gradually build perseverance by choosing challenges that are just a fraction beyond what the child is already able to do. As success mounts, steps can be made larger.

Choosing challenges that are too easy. Parents and children may come to therapy with the mistaken notion that the child must always be comfortable. This idea causes them to shy away from even moderately challenging exposures. Initially, the therapist might allow small steps to build trust in the process, with the aim of encouraging larger leaps of faith over time.

Progressing too quickly, or too slowly. Unfortunately, there is not a set pace that works for all children. Motivation, distress tolerance, and frequency of practice all influence readiness to move to the next level of an exposure hierarchy. Some therapists dictate the pace, recommending moving up every fourth day, for example, or after a challenge has been done three times. Others use a Subjective Units of Distress Scale (SUDS) to keep the child in that sweet spot of just outside their comfort zone. Aim for a pace that is neither hurried nor languid, frequently referring to "next steps" so both the child and parent remember that exposure is dynamic.

The child is unwittingly undoing exposure with safety behaviors. It is not unusual for children to fall back on safety behaviors in an effort to reduce the anxiety stirred up by exposure. For example, a child may seek reassurance in the midst of an exposure, or they might throw themself into activity to distract from what they are doing. Keep in mind that self-regulation strategies can morph into safety behaviors as well. Getting rid of safety behaviors is the response prevention side of ERP, and an important thing to check if therapy is stalling.

Resistance on the part of the child. Children are more inclined to participate in exposure when they feel safe, seen, and heard by the therapist. Take the time to establish rapport. Give the child choices whenever possible. Start small, imparting early success. Focus on issues that matter to the child first, even if they differ from the parents' priorities. Address resistance when you see it, and work to increase trust, confidence, and motivation.

Resistance on the part of the parent. As much as they genuinely want their child to feel better, some parents hold beliefs that get in the way of exposure. Thinking it's their job to keep their child "comfortable" is one such belief. Seeing anxiety as dangerous is another. Not making time for exposure, or doing it in a rushed or punitive way, will also cause progress to falter. Parents might need additional support to be able to implement exposures at home and to coach their child effectively.

Underlying comorbidity. Comorbidity itself isn't necessarily the problem; failure to take it into account is. Always begin with a comprehensive assessment so you know about underlying medical, learning, sensory, behavioral, and emotional issues as all impact the child's experience of the world and their ability to be successful in treatment.

HOW IS THIS BOOK ORGANIZED?

Assuming you've done a thorough evaluation, determined that ERP is the right intervention, and established a treatment plan, you are ready to use *The A–Z Guide*. If, for example, you and the family have prioritized falling asleep independently, you would flip to *Sleeping Alone*.

Efforts have been made to include common search terms, resulting in primary and secondary listings. Under each primary listing, you will see Considerations, or factors to keep in mind about the topic, followed by a list of exposures, which move from easier to harder challenges. The first sentence of each exposure is directed to the child. For example, under *Asymmetry*, one of the exposures reads, "Play **Simon Says**," followed by further instructions for the therapist. Where applicable, the text following exposures suggests ways to modify or escalate the challenge.

Secondary listings direct you to primary listings. For example, if you are treating a child who is afraid of needles and you look up *Needles*, *Jabs*, or *Shots*, you will find *See: Injections*. Synonyms for *Injections* are secondary headings, while *Injections* is the primary listing that contains the list of exposures.

Frequently co-occurring fears are listed after many of the primary headings on a line that begins with Also. For example, after looking at the exposures for *Baddies (fictional)*, you will see, *Also: Navigating Home Alone, Separation Anxiety, Sleeping Alone, Uncertainty, Words and Phrases*. If you flip to any of those listings, you will find exposures for these commonly related issues.

A few last things: assume that the child is performing the exposure activity, unless otherwise indicated. Remember that exposure is best done with a supportive adult, most typically a parent or therapist. Some of the activities in this guide might seem too easy for the child you are working with, a few might not seem relevant. Work with the child and parent to personalize the list, then have the child sort from least to most scary. Decide together on the best starting point. Practice in the session or assign as homework, and you'll be on your way.

We wish you all the best in your ERP endeavors!

—Dawn & Erin

A–Z GUIDE

A

ADDICTION
See: Drugs

AIRPLANES
See: Contamination, Crowded Places, Flying, Motion Sickness, Panic, Vomiting

ALARMS
See: Noises

ALCOHOL/ALCOHOLISM
See: Drugs

ALIENS
See: Baddies

ALONE
See: Navigating Home Alone, Separation Anxiety

ANIMALS
See: Bees, Birds, Bugs, Dangerous Animals, Dogs, Frogs, Pet Escaping

ANTS
See: Bugs

APOLOGIES

Considerations

There is debate about whether or not to insist on having children make apologies. There are also varying opinions about whether it is important for the child to mean it, or if simply saying "I'm sorry" is enough. We know that apologies work to repair relationships, and that sincere apologies are healing for both the giver and receiver. While a heartfelt apology is the end goal, smaller steps may be needed to master this important life skill.

When talking to a child about a rift that has occurred in a relationship, start by asking if they feel ready to make things better. If they say "Yes," great! Support the child as they figure out how to do this, including what they might say by way of apology. If the child indicates or directly says "No," remain empathic. Say, "I hear you. It can be hard to apologize, especially when you still feel angry." Help the child manage their feelings, then try again.

Exposures

○ Do something to show you care.
  When apologizing is too difficult, coach the parent to put what is happening into words, "It looks like saying *I'm sorry* is too hard right now. What can we do to show [the person] you care?" The parent can offer relationship-mending gestures such as shaking hands, a hug, or doing the person a favor.

○ Read a book about a character who makes a mistake and apologizes.

○ Draw or write a note of apology.
  Move from mailing an "I'm sorry" note or drawing to having the child hand deliver it. Increase the challenge over subsequent apologies by having the child remain present, and eventually make eye contact, while their note is being opened.

○ Tell the apology to an adult, who then delivers it for you.
  Move from the child being absent when their apology is conveyed to being present, and eventually, making eye contact.

○ Record an apology.
  Move from sending the recorded apology electronically to having the child present while it is being played.

○ Apologize in person.
  Consider starting with the child apologizing out of view, for example

A

standing back-to-back or behind something before moving to apologizing face-to-face.

O Increase the volume of a spoken apology, moving from a whisper to a full voice.

O Start with a simple apology.
Move from a simple, "I'm sorry" to a more complete apology that includes what the child is sorry for, why they are sorry, and what they will do differently next time.

Also: Mistakes, Perfectionism, Social Anxiety

ASYMMETRY
Considerations
The compulsion to make things symmetrical often occurs in the context of OCD alongside the need to have things feel "just right." Exposure aims to have the child immerse themself in asymmetry on purpose, inducing, but not giving in to, the urge to make things right.

Exposures

O Delay making things even.
When the urge to make something symmetrical strikes, coach the child to insert a several-second delay. Increase the delay over time, working toward 30-minutes as by then, the urge is likely to vanish.

O Play **Simon Says**.
Take turns as "Simon," with directions such as, "Simon says, touch your left leg. Simon says, touch both feet. Simon says, hop on one foot. Now stop." Be sure to leave many of the directives one-sided to help the child practice tolerating asymmetry.

O Walk or run using different-sized steps.

O Tilt pictures on the wall so they are crooked.
If necessary, move from quickly tilting and fixing the pictures to tilting and leaving them that way.

○ Practice making things uneven on purpose.
For example, if the child inadvertently clinks their spoon against one side of a bowl, and then clinks the other side to make it even, have the child clink the first side again to make it uneven on purpose.

○ Wear mismatched socks.
Challenge the child to wear socks with different colors, patterns, heights, or textures, or to pull up one and scrunch the other sock down.

○ Wear uneven accessories.
For example, have the child wear a watch or bracelet on just one wrist, two different earrings, a scarf draped unevenly, or a hat tilted to one side.

○ Use an **Uneven Challenge Jar**.
Put together an Uneven Challenge Jar. Each day, the child can pull a new challenge from the jar. For short challenges, they can roll a die to determine how many times to do it. Sample challenges might include: "Pull one sock all the way up"; "Walk through a doorway, brushing the left side of your body against the wall"; "Touch your nose with your right pinky"; or "Give a one-armed hug."

○ Put **Body Art** on one side of your body.
Have the child apply a fake tattoo, or draw or write on a frequently seen body part. Increase the time the art stays in place. Make the challenge more difficult with asymmetrical or otherwise imperfect art, such as including a misspelled word, a backward letter, or a messy shape.

Uneven Challenge Jar

✓ Wear different colored socks.

✓ Wear socks that pull up to different heights.

✓ Fix hair in an asymmetrical style. Mix a ponytail with a braid or a thick braid with a thin one. Clip up just one side or wear a crooked part. Brush a portion of the hair forward and gel the rest of it back.

✓ Wear bands on one wrist but not the other.

✓ Trail just one hand along the wall as you walk down a hallway.

✓ Eat in an asymmetrical way. For example, if eating blueberries, sometimes put one in your mouth, sometimes two, sometimes three. Chew on only one side of your mouth. Bite into some blueberries as you are putting them in your mouth, but not others.

✓ Rub lotion into just one hand.

✓ Give a one-armed hug.

✓ Rub one hand up and down one thigh.

✓ Give a one-handed high five.

✓ Sit off-center.

✓ Pull the shades to different heights.

✓ Leave one fingernail longer than the others.

✓ Lean against something with one side of your body.

✓ Walk with uneven steps.

✓ Hang a name sign on your door, making the letters uneven.

✓ Draw a picture to hang in your house, making it uneven on purpose.

✓ Move objects on your desk or dresser so they no longer line up.

○ Mislace one shoe on purpose.
Have the child mislace one shoe or tie their shoes differently, increasing the time they leave it that way over subsequent exposures.

○ Do things with the wrong hand.
Have the child do daily activities such as eating and brushing teeth with their non-dominant hand.

○ Smudge something on purpose.
Have the child make a smudge or other small mark on one side of a device screen or eyeglasses, then leave it there.

Also: Just Right Feeling, Mistakes

ATTIC
See: Baddies, Dark, Navigating Home Alone

A

B

BAD GUYS
See: Baddies

BADDIES (FICTIONAL)
Considerations
This category includes malevolent fictional people and characters including witches, monsters, vampires, ghosts, aliens, dolls that come to life, and urban legends. "Scary" fictional characters from books and movies can be included as well, along with real-life baddies who are deceased, so they can't possibly pose a threat.

When treating fears of fictional baddies, craft exposures for both the character and the activities of daily living the child is avoiding. Exposure to the scary character is covered in this section, while exposure to activities like Navigating Home Alone and Sleeping Alone can be found under those headings.

Exposures

○ Say the name of the baddie.
  Have the child move from whispering the name, to saying it louder, to shouting it.

○ Read the name of the baddie.
  Have the child move from reading it silently to reading it out loud.

○ Write the name of the baddie.
  Have the child move from writing and immediately erasing the name to writing and displaying it.

○ Make an **Acrostic** of the baddie's name.
  Have the child write the name of the baddie vertically on a page, then write an adjective describing the baddie starting with each letter.

○ Look at pictures of the baddie.
Encourage the child to move from quick glimpses to sustained looking. Eventually hang the picture somewhere.

○ Doodle on a picture of the baddie.
Using a picture the child has drawn or one an adult finds and prints, have the child modify the picture to make it silly by drawing on funny clothing, a goofy scene, or people interacting with the baddie.

○ Do a puzzle of the baddie.
Cut up a picture of the baddie and give the pieces to the child to assemble.

○ Write a limerick about the baddie.
Limericks are funny poems that have an AABBA rhyming pattern. The idea is to think about the baddie in creative, silly ways.

○ Make up a story about the baddie.
Help the child invent a backstory about the baddie by asking questions such as: "What does the baddie eat for breakfast?" "What kind of underwear do they wear?" "Do they own a pet?" "What is their middle name?" "What embarrasses them?" Move from silly or benign stories to scarier stories.

○ Find or make a model of the baddie.
Give the child supplies such as clay, paper mache, or cloth to make a model of the baddie.

○ Use a picture of the baddie as a screensaver or device wallpaper.

○ Visit a picture of the baddie in a store.
Check party stores, costume stores, and bookstores for images of the baddie. Over subsequent exposures, have the child move closer to the picture of the baddie, first with the parent, then alone. Challenge the child to touch the image of the baddie, then take a selfie with it.

○ Play **News Reporter**.
Help the child to write a journalistic story about the baddie. Consider: What is their favorite snack? What kind of pet do they have? How do they celebrate their birthday? What embarrasses them? What's something they are really bad at? Who invented this baddie and why?

○ Make a music video starring the baddie.

B

○ Say the name of the baddie while alone in a room.
Over subsequent exposures, increase the number of times the child says the name of the baddie, then increase the amount of time the child stays alone in the room. You can also have the child write the name of the baddie while alone in a room.

○ Draw the baddie or look at pictures of them while alone in a room.
Challenge the child to think about what is scary about the baddie while looking at a picture of them. Extend the time the child stays in the room alone after purposely thinking about the baddie, allowing them to draw, read a book, or do another unrelated activity after they have thought about the baddie. Avoid the use of electronics, which are so absorbing that they take away from the effectiveness of this exposure.

Also: Navigating Home Alone, Separation Anxiety, Sleeping Alone, Uncertainty, Words and Phrases

BADDIES (REAL LIFE)
Considerations

Children sometimes become preoccupied with people who inflict harm on others, including intruders, robbers, kidnappers, and terrorists. Therapists get involved when these fears exist out of proportion to the actual danger. For example, the child in a safe neighborhood who won't go upstairs alone because there might be a kidnapper, or won't play outside for fear of terrorists. Treatment in these instances exposes the child to the activities they are avoiding, not the baddies themselves. So, exposure may focus on navigating the home, reducing reassurance-seeking, or sleeping alone.

In addition to impacting daily activities, a fear of baddies can spread to people who are not dangerous but may be naively considered so, such as teenagers, people with addictions, or people who wear certain clothes. Exposure to real-world people who are seen as dangerous even though they are not is covered under Differentness.

See: Crowded Places, Differentness, Navigating Home Alone, Separation Anxiety, Sleeping Alone, Uncertainty

B

BALLOONS
Considerations
The fear of balloons is almost always centered on the possibility that the balloon will pop. This fear can be surprisingly limiting when, for example, it becomes impossible for the child to attend birthday parties, go into stores that sell party supplies, go to sporting events, or frequent venues that might have balloons. Because popping is a distinct possibility, exposure does culminate in watching, listening to, causing, and being surprised by the popping of balloons.

Exposures

O Draw pictures of balloons.

O Do a balloon **Word Search**.
There are websites that will create a Word Search for you from relevant keywords such as: float, birthday, pop, squeak, boom, static, inflate, or tie.

O Look at pictures of balloons.
Start with drawings, then move to photos. Go from deflated to inflated balloons.

O Sit near an empty balloon.
Have the child move from sitting near the deflated balloon, to holding it, to stretching it.

O Make a balloon stress ball.
Have the child put a funnel in a balloon and fill it with flour, corn starch, or sand, and tie it off.

O Play **Catch** with a water balloon.
Start with just a little water and work toward playing Catch with a full water balloon.

O Play with a balloon.
Begin by partially inflating the balloon. Tie it off and play with it. Gradually move toward fully inflating the balloon, tying it off and playing with it. Drawing on the balloon beforehand makes this activity more fun.

O Draw on a balloon.
Have the child draw on an empty balloon, then blow it up to see what it looks like. Or draw designs or faces on inflated balloons.

O Let an untied balloon whizz around the room.

B

○ Play **Keep It Up**.
Blow up a balloon and take turns patting it back into the air using your hand or an implement. Moving from a semi-inflated to fully inflated balloon will make this exposure more challenging.

○ Have a **Balloon Spoon Race**.
Race to the finish with an inflated balloon balanced on a large spoon.

○ Make a balloon-powered vehicle.
Working together with the child, attach a balloon to a straw, then tape it to the top of a makeshift car such as a juice box, water bottle, or small toy vehicle. Use a stick for the axles, and attach wheels. Blow into the balloon, release it, and watch the car go!

○ Make balloon animals.
Make animals with the child, or spell their name with long, thin balloons. Work toward having the child keep the balloon art in their room.

○ Watch balloons popping online.
Start by watching with the sound off. Gradually increase the sound over time until full volume is achieved. Add fun by watching the videos forward and backward.

○ Pop a balloon.
Start with a partially inflated balloon, which will make a less dramatic sound. Work up to popping a fully inflated balloon. Have the child pop the balloon in a variety of ways: with a pin, by sitting on it, or as part of a race. Hiding small toys or treats in the balloons beforehand will make this exposure more fun.

○ Stay nearby while someone else pops a balloon.
Move from having the child do a countdown before the balloon is popped to less predictable popping, which adds the key ingredients of suspense and surprise. Increase proximity to the balloon over time.

○ Have a **Balloon Knee Race**.
Place a balloon between each runner's knees. Whoever passes the finish line first, with the balloon still between their knees, wins.

○ Play **Guard Your Balloon**.
Tie strings to full balloons, then tie one to each player's ankle. Players try to pop each other's balloon by squeezing, sitting, or stepping on it. The winner is the last person with an un-popped balloon.

Also: Noises

B

BASEMENT

See: Baddies, Bugs, Dark, Navigating Home Alone

BATHROOM

See: Navigating Home Alone, Noises, Toileting, Wiping

BEES

Considerations

It bears repeating that many childhood fears make sense. Stings hurt! We want children to be cautious around stinging insects. But only a tiny fraction of the bees, wasps, hornets, and yellowjackets we encounter are actually going to sting us. So, taking extreme measures to avoid this minute possibility is both limiting and unnecessary. We want the child to play outside and navigate all of the places they might encounter stinging insects. We want them to use caution without panicking when they actually see one. It will take many, many instances of being around stinging insects without getting stung for the child to learn that their fear is a false alarm. While we largely use the word *bee*, the following exposures can be used for any stinging insect the child fears.

Exposures

○ Make a list of stinging insects.
  Work with the child to create a list of stinging insects, then have them organize it from the least to the most scary.

○ Do a bee **Word Search**.
  There are websites that will create a Word Search from relevant keywords. The child can search for words like: stinger, yellow, flying, honey, queen, worker, wings, pollen, or hive.

○ Look at pictures of bees.
  Move from cartoon drawings to photos and from benign-seeming to creepier-looking bees.

○ Draw bees.

○ Watch videos of bees.

○ Write a story about a bee.

B

- Write a song about a bee.

- Make a stop-motion animation about a bee.

- Make bee arts and crafts.
  Provide supplies for the child to create finger-puppets, pipe-cleaner bees, pasta bees, bee masks, or clay bees, making sure to include supplies for the stinger.

- Play with toy bees.
  Play with the child, acting out scenarios involving bees flying, crawling, and landing on people.

- Decorate pictures of bees.
  Print out pictures of bees. Have the child draw on them, adding clothing, hats, and scenes around them. Start with cartoonish, benign-looking bees and move to more realistic ones.

- Do a bee puzzle.
  Use a bee puzzle or make one by printing an image of bees and cutting it into puzzle shapes for the child to assemble.

- Hang pictures of bees around the home.

- Find a picture of bees to use as a device screensaver or wallpaper.

- Read illustrated fact books about bees.

- Play **Catch** with toy bees.

- Play **Find It**, taking turns hiding and finding toy bees.

- Play **Gotcha!**
  Have the family take turns hiding toy bees around the home. When someone finds one, they get to re-hide it, which means that eventually the child will start encountering plastic bees in unexpected places. Realistic toy bees will make this game more challenging.

- Hold a dead bee.
  Have the child start at a comfortable distance and move closer over time. Let the child observe someone else holding the dead bee. Over subsequent exposures, have the child touch the dead bee, then hold it themselves.

B

○ Spend time outside, in places known for bees.
Start with the amount of time you know the child can tolerate, offering a fun outdoor activity. If necessary, begin in a place the child is unlikely to encounter a bee before moving to a garden, park or other spot more likely to contain bees. Gradually increase the time spent in each location while moving away from highly compelling distractions.

○ Go to a science museum or zoo with an entomology exhibit.
Have the child practice getting closer to the bees.

○ Look at a live bee in a jar.
Have an adult collect a live bee in a jar. The child can look at the bee in the jar from a distance before moving closer and eventually, over subsequent exposures, holding the jar.

○ Look at bees from a distance.
Binoculars, if available, add an element of fun while allowing the child to watch bees from further away. Decrease the distance over time.

○ Play **Spot It!**
Whoever points out the most bees wins.

○ Go on a **Bee Scavenger Hunt**.
The list could include Find a Bee: near a flower, near a garbage pail, flying, crawling, that is fuzzy, that is long.

○ Go on a **Bee Photo Safari**.
Have the child take pictures of bees, experimenting with creative angles and close-ups.

Bee Scavenger Hunt

Find a...

✔ Plant that is taller than you
✔ Bee, wasp, hornet, or yellowjacket
✔ Flower that smells good
✔ Flat rock
✔ Stinging insect on a flower
✔ Bench
✔ Pair of stinging insects
✔ Leaf on the ground
✔ Ant
✔ Rock that sparkles
✔ Bee, wasp, hornet, or yellowjacket that is flying
✔ Something a bee would like
✔ Flying insect that doesn't sting
✔ Seed or pod
✔ Feather

○ Play **Bee Bingo**.
A Bingo card could include: a bumble bee, a wasp, a hornet, a bee hive, a bee on a flower, or a bee in the grass. Reward the completion of rows, then the whole card.

○ Visit an apiary.
Take a tour to learn about beekeeping. Whoever is accompanying the child should first talk to the beekeeper about the child's fear of bees.

Also: Dangerous Animals

B

BIRDS

Considerations

The fear of birds might center on a particular type of bird, or extend to all birds. Sometimes the fear has to do with the lack of predictability or the possibility of attack. Make sure you understand the nature and scope of the fear before initiating exposure. Also keep in mind that the child is likely to come across birds in their natural environment, which means that in addition to planned exposure, it is best to create a protocol for unplanned encounters.

Exposures

- Make a list of birds.
  Have the child make a list either alone or with a supportive adult, then circle the birds that seem scary.

- Play the **Alphabet Game** with birds.
  For example: A-Albatross, B-Blackbird, C-Chickadee…

- Draw birds.

- Make bird arts and crafts.
  Have the child create bird finger-puppets, pipe-cleaner birds, pasta birds, bird masks, or clay birds.

- Look at pictures of birds.
  Start with cartoon images and move toward photos.

- Draw on pictures of birds.
  Print pictures of birds found online. Have the child draw on them, adding silly clothing, additional birds, or scenes around them.

- Write a story about a bird. Make a stop-motion animation of the story.

- Write a haiku about a bird.

- Make or buy a cuddly bird toy.

- Use a picture of a bird as a device screensaver or wallpaper.

- Read illustrated fact books about birds.

- Play **Catch** with toy birds.

- Play **Find It**, taking turns hiding and finding toy birds.

B

○ Play **Gotcha!**
Take turns hiding toy birds around the home. When someone finds a bird, they get to re-hide it, which means that eventually the child will start encountering birds in unexpected places. Realistic toy birds will make this game more challenging.

○ Do a bird puzzle.
Buy or make a puzzle by printing an image of birds and cutting it into puzzle shapes for the child to assemble.

○ Hang pictures of birds around the home.
Begin with less scary birds the child has drawn, moving toward photos of birds, including those the child finds scary.

○ Listen to bird sounds.
Find audio of bird sounds. Start by doing an activity while the sound plays at low volume in the background, then move to listening at full volume and without distraction.

○ Watch videos of birds.
Start with short clips of less scary birds before moving to longer videos of feared birds.

○ Find birds in nature.
Use binoculars to watch from a distance, then move closer. Talk about what each bird is doing and ask the child to predict where it might go next.

○ Play **Spot It!**
Whoever spots the first bird wins. Play multiple rounds in various settings.

○ Go on a **Bird Scavenger Hunt**.
Items might include Find a Bird: near a flower, that is flying, that is brown, that is eating, that is walking, that is colorful.

○ Play **Bird Bingo**.
Include items such as: a cardinal, a birdfeeder, a blackbird, a bird in the water, or a bird flying. Reward completion of a row, then the entire card.

○ Go on a **Bird Photo Safari**.
Have the child experiment with different angles and close-ups.

○ Hang a bird feeder near your home.

B

○ Visit someone's home who has a pet bird.
  Begin by having the bird in another room during the visit. Then visit with the bird in the same room in their cage. If possible, move to being in a room with the bird out of its cage.

○ Visit an aviary, zoo, or bird sanctuary.
  Challenge the child to get closer to the birds over time.

BLOOD

Considerations

When treating an intense fear of blood, it is important to understand why the fear has surfaced. Some children develop this fear as a result of an injury, abuse, or trauma. Others have an anticipatory fear of pain. The child might also experience vasovagal syncope, which causes a person to faint at the sight of blood. Understanding the cause of the child's fear will help you decide between exposure or more trauma-informed care.

Exposures

○ Write the word *blood*.
  Initially allow the child to immediately erase the word, cross it out, or throw it away. Move toward having the child write *blood* in block letters to decorate and display.

○ Say the word *blood*.
  Increase exposure by having the child say *blood* in various voices such as: a baby voice, a lion's voice, a loud voice, a whisper voice, or their favorite character's voice. The child can also roll two dice and then say *blood* that number of times.

○ Make up a story about blood.
  Both the child and adult can contribute details to the story. Stories can be funny or serious, realistic or fanciful. Be sure the word *blood* appears many times in the story.

○ Draw bleeding people.
  Have the child use red to make the blood stand out.

○ Look at pictures of bleeding people.
  Pre-select appropriate photos to avoid unnecessarily gruesome images.

B

○ Put fake blood on your body.
Begin with a red marker then move to making fake blood. Let the child put the blood first on someone else's body, then on their own.

○ Act out injuries with fake blood.
Film the child pretending to get hurt. Add fake blood. Watch the movie together, forward and backward, in fast, slow, and regular motion.

> **Recipe for Fake Blood**
>
> 1 tbsp corn syrup
>
> a couple drops of red food coloring
>
> a touch of cocoa (optional)

○ Watch videos of blood draws and minor injuries. Start with someone different from the child in terms of gender, age, or nationality. Progress to a more similar person. Titrate the amount of blood that is visible in the video. An adult should prescreen videos.

○ Squeeze out a drop of your own blood.
Allow the child to watch an adult prick and squeeze their own finger first, starting from far away or with only one eye open if necessary. Over time, have the child prick and then squeeze their own finger. Eventually make the challenge more difficult by having the child touch their own blood before covering the spot with a bandage.

Also: Dentists, Doctors, Health, Injections, Words and Phrases

BOATS
Considerations
When treating children who avoid boats due to motion sickness, remember that the target for exposure is being in a boat, not feeling ill. There are supportive strategies to help motion-sick children be more comfortable, including wearing motion sickness bands, keeping eyes on the horizon, and staying out of choppy water. If the fear is related to something other than motion sickness, such as falling overboard, address boat safety while doing the following exposures. Teach parents to gradually withdraw and eventually eliminate reassurance about boats.

Exposures

○ Look at pictures of boats.

○ Make a collage of pictures of boats.

B

○ Read a fact book about boats.

○ Watch videos of boats moving.
Collect a variety of videos that allow the child to see the boat moving from different perspectives including from shore, from another boat, and from the deck of the boat.

○ Write a story about someone having an adventure on a boat.

○ Make toy boats and float them on water.

○ Watch a movie that includes boats.
Prescreen to select an appropriate level of exposure, moving from animated to realistic movies and from small to larger boats. Eventually include the type of boat the child most fears. Do not show boating disasters as this will work against the purpose of exposure.

○ Listen to a pretend story about riding on a boat.
Do a detailed imaginal exposure of the child taking a boat ride, with the therapist or parent narrating.

○ Play a video game that involves boats.
Consider gaming console games, virtual reality games, and online games. They should be prescreened, with the amount of exposure carefully chosen by the therapist.

○ Visit a marina to watch boats coming and going.
Challenge the child to move closer to the boats over time.

○ Walk onto a docked boat.
Have the child do an activity on the boat, staying long enough to get used to the motion of the boat on the water.

○ Take a short boat ride.
Start with an amount of time that feels only slightly uncomfortable to the child, even if only a few seconds, gradually extending the time over subsequent exposures.

Also: Dangerous Animals, Motion Sickness, Panic, Uncertainty, Vomiting, Water Immersion

BOOKS
See: Baddies, Media

B

BOWEL MOVEMENTS
See: Contamination, Health, Toileting, Uncertainty, Wiping

BUGS
Considerations
It is normal to feel apprehensive about bugs. They appear out of nowhere and often act in unpredictable ways. But when apprehension rises to the level of a phobia complete with extreme fear or avoidance of daily activities and places, it is time to consider exposure.

Some children are afraid of a particular kind of bug, others fear bugs more broadly. In either case, it is best to begin exposure with bugs the child sees as benign, or at least less scary, such as ladybugs, ants, or butterflies.

Exposures

O Make a list of bugs that live around you.
   Have the child organize the list from the least to the most scary.

O Play the **Alphabet Game** with bugs as the category.
   For example: A-Ant, B-Bee, C-Caterpillar...

O Make bug snacks.
   Make fun treats that look like insects, such as black cookies with licorice legs for spiders, peanut butter filled celery topped with raisins for ants on a log, or butterflies with apple slice wings and carrot bodies. Talk about bugs while eating.

O Look at pictures of bugs.
   Move from cartoon drawings to photos and from attractive to creepier-looking bugs.

O Read a book with bug characters.

O Draw the bugs that scare you.

O Make bug arts and crafts.
   Have the child create bug finger-puppets, pipe-cleaner bugs, pasta bugs, bug masks, egg carton bugs, or clay bugs.

O Write a story about a bug.

O Write a song about a bug.

B

- Make a stop-motion animation about a bug.

- Play bug games.
  Find board games or online games that involve bugs.

- Play with toy bugs.
  Play with the child, acting out stories that include bugs flying, crawling, and landing on people, as well as bugs popping up unexpectedly.

- Draw on pictures of bugs.
  Print pictures of bugs and have the child draw on them, adding clothing, hats, and scenes. Start with cartoonish, benign looking bugs before moving to more realistic or "scary" bugs.

- Do a bug puzzle.
  Buy or make a puzzle by printing an image of bugs and cutting it into puzzle shapes for the child to assemble.

- Hang bug art.
  Print pictures or draw bugs and hang them around the home.

- Use a picture of bugs as a device screensaver or wallpaper.

- Read illustrated fact books about bugs.

- Play **Memory** with bug pictures.
  Print pairs of pictures of bugs, cutting them to make similar-size cards. Take turns turning over two cards at a time, trying to find pairs.

- Play **Catch** with toy bugs.

- Play **Find It**, taking turns hiding and finding a toy bug.

- Play **Gotcha!**
  Take turns hiding toy bugs around the home. When someone finds a bug, they get to re-hide it, which means that eventually the child will start encountering fake bugs in unexpected places. Realistic toy bugs will make this game more challenging.

- Look at dead bugs.
  Start at a comfortable distance and have the child move closer over time.

- Hold a dead bug.
  The child may need to start by observing someone else holding the dead bug before they can hold it themself.

B

○ Spend time outdoors in places where there might be bugs.
Begin with an amount of time you know the child can tolerate, offering a fun activity. Gradually increase the time spent outside while moving away from highly compelling distractions.

○ Collect dead bugs.

○ Go to a science museum or zoo with an entomology exhibit.
Practice getting closer to the bugs.

○ Do a **Color Card Scavenger Hunt**.
Using green and brown paint samples from a paint or hardware store, challenge the child to find those exact colors in nature. Move to having the child find bugs in those colors.

○ Go on a **Bug Scavenger Hunt**.
Include items such as Find a Bug: on a leaf, that flies, that is green, that is tiny, or that is near another bug.

○ Go on a **Bug Photo Safari**.
Have the child take pictures of bugs, experimenting with creative angles and close-ups.

○ Scoop up live bugs outside.
Begin by using an implement such as a butterfly net or piece of paper, then move to using hands. Make contests such as: Who can catch the most bugs in a minute? Who can move a bug from here to there the fastest? Who can let a bug crawl furthest up their arm?

○ Get a pet bug or ant farm.
Have the child help with caretaking.

Also: Bees

BUTTONS
Considerations
Extreme discomfort with buttoned clothing is more common than you might think. If you suspect a child is avoiding buttons due to difficulty with fine motor skills or broader sensory sensitivities, refer to Occupational Therapy for evaluation. Sometimes avoidance of buttons morphs into discomfort and refusal, becoming problematic when the child needs to get dressed up, wear a sports uniform, or put on a buttoned coat. At its most extreme, children with button

B

phobias cannot tolerate being in the same room as a person wearing buttons. Fortunately, exposure to buttons is quite straightforward, making this phobia relatively easy to treat.

Exposures

O Say the word *button*.
Encourage the child to play with the word, saying it fast and slow, in different tones of voice or accents.

O Write the word *button*.
Have the child use print, cursive, or bubble letters to make a button poster.

O Draw buttons of all shapes and sizes.

O Do a **Hidden Picture** activity related to buttons.

O Play **Tic-Tac-Toe** using different buttons as playing pieces.

O Look at pictures of clothing that has buttons.

O Use a picture of buttons as a device screensaver or wallpaper.

O Have a **Button Shoe Race**.
Rest a button on each person's shoe. Walk as fast as possible, keeping the button balanced on the shoe. Whoever reaches the finish line first wins.

O Hold a loose button.
Start with an amount of time the child finds tolerable, even if only a second. Extend the time over subsequent exposures until the child is holding and even playing with the button.

O See how far you can roll a button across a table.

O Play **Catch** with a button.

O Play **Cup Toss** with a button.
Lay out several cups and see who can get the most buttons in.

O Use buttons to practice math skills.

O Use buttons for arts and crafts.
String buttons to create a necklace. Glue buttons onto a piece of paper so they become scoops of ice cream or a bouquet of flowers, or spell the child's name. Pin buttons to a styrofoam ball to create an ornament. Be creative!

B

○ Build a tower with buttons.

○ Play **Find It**, taking turns hiding and finding buttons.
Move from hiding individual buttons to hiding clothing with buttons. Over subsequent rounds of the game, increase the challenge by requiring the finder to put on the clothing and run to a designated spot.

○ Play **Memory** with buttons.
Hide matching pairs of buttons under plastic cups. Take turns lifting the cups to find matches.

○ Hold a jar filled with buttons.
Start at whatever distance the child can tolerate, progressively moving closer to the jar and eventually holding it. Have the child guess how many buttons are in the jar. Increase the challenge by having the child plunge their hand into the jar. Time them to see how long they can keep their hand in the jar, wiggling their fingers in the buttons.

○ Look at a buttoned shirt.
Hang a buttoned shirt first in a common area, then in the child's room. Over subsequent exposures, have the child move closer to the shirt and eventually touch it. Extend the length of time the child stays in the room with the shirt.

○ Do an activity with a buttoned shirt in your lap.
Have the child do an activity such as drawing, reading, or playing cards with a buttoned shirt lying across their lap.

○ Learn how to sew on a button.

○ Wear a piece of clothing with buttons.
Have the child put the clothing on without fastening the buttons. Over subsequent exposures, move to buttoning and immediately unbuttoning the clothing. Work toward putting the clothing on, buttoning it, and wearing it for an extended period of time. At any level of this exposure, you can add an element of fun by challenging the child to do certain things while wearing the item of clothing. Examples include wacky relay races that involve taking a button shirt off and putting it back on, holding a mis-match fashion show, or making up clapping games that can only be played while buttons are buttoned.

B

CARS
See: Motion Sickness, Vomiting

CATS
See: Dogs, Pet Escaping

CELLAR
See: Baddies, Bugs, Dark, Navigating Home Alone

CHALLENGES
See: Making Decisions, Mistakes, Trying New Things

CHANGE IN PLANS
Considerations
Children with Autism Spectrum Disorder (ASD) or children with a rigid cognitive style often need support and practice adapting to change. Interventions such as written or picture schedules, frequent cueing, and self-regulation strategies should be used in combination with exposure. Neurotypical children who feel anxious when things change benefit from these techniques, too. Exposure to changes in plans helps children habituate to everyday changes, reducing the likelihood of anxious or angry responses.

Exposures

○ Drive a new way to a place you know well.
   Encourage parents to purposely vary driving routes, telling the child ahead of time to make clear that this is an exposure.

○ Read something the wrong way.
Have the child intentionally mispronounce words, read from the end of the book to the beginning, or read "wrong" in other ways. An adult reading to the child can intentionally make these "mistakes," too.

○ Set up a room in a different way.
Some children will need to start very slowly, varying the throw pillows in a seldom-used room, for example, or moving a chair to a slightly different spot. Move toward making larger changes to rooms that matter more to the child, remembering that exposure is best done with a child, not to them.

○ Say hello or good-bye in a different way.
Encourage key adults to vary greetings and good-byes, especially if the child is ritualistic and wants them to be the same every time.

○ Play with different toys.
Have parents periodically rotate which toys are available for play. This exposure is not about purchasing new toys but rather teaching children to vary which toys they are playing with.

○ Sit someplace different.
Have the child sit in a different spot in the car, at the dinner table, or while watching TV. Make a game out of this by introducing chance, rolling a die or spinning a home-made spinner to determine where the child will sit.

○ Play **Change It Up**.
Begin by talking about doing things differently, for example, "What would happen if we drove home a new way?" or "What would it be like to eat dessert first?" Then, flip a coin to decide whether or not to "change it up" and follow the alternative plan.

Change It Up Questions

"What would it be like to drive a different route to school?"

"What would it be like to eat dessert first?"

"What would it be like to brush your teeth with your other hand?"

"What would it be like to go to the park instead of home after school?"

"What would it be like to stop for gas on the way home?"

"What would it be like to brush your hair before instead of after breakfast?"

"What would it be like to play a new game?"

"What would it be like to read a different number of books at bedtime?"

"What would it be like to drink water out of a coffee cup?"

"What would it be like to say good-bye differently?"

"What would it be like to sleep in a different bedroom?"

"What would it be like to hold the door for everyone?"

"What would it be like to wear your shirt backward?"

"What would it be like to sit on the floor to eat?"

"What would it be like to have a conversation with our backs to each other?"

"What would it be like to switch chores?"

C

○ Let someone else lead play.
During play and with a light attitude, the therapist or parent can play with a character the child identifies as theirs, move objects the child has placed, introduce new characters, or incorporate new storylines.

○ Play **Fast Again, Slow Again**.
During an imaginary play activity such as school or store, take turns periodically shouting, "Fast Again!" or "Slow Again!" to change the speed of play.

○ Try a different brand of a food you like.

○ Eat foods you like in new ways.
Parents can, for example, cut a sandwich into three parts rather than four or slice bread on the diagonal.

○ Go on a **Mystery Drive**.
Have the child go on a ride without knowing where they are going. Begin with fun end-points such as an ice cream shop or the library. Move toward more routine stops such as the grocery store or gas station.

○ Change routines.
Teach parents to intentionally, and with notice, vary common routines. For example, if one parent always supervises bathtime, have the other parent do it. Begin by telling the child in advance who is going to help them, then move to an arbitrary way of deciding, such as flipping a coin or deciding at the last minute.

○ Flip a coin to make choices.
Use an arbitrary method, such as flipping a coin, to decide what to play, who goes first, who sits in the front seat, or who picks the movie.

○ Practice changing the plan.
Work with the family to decide how many days a week to practice changing a plan. On the designated days, have the parent start the day by reminding the child, "Today's the day I'm going to change a plan." Remind the child closer to the actual change, and again at the time of the change. Start small with things like which section of the library to visit first, what to have for dinner, or where to go after school. Increase the challenge by decreasing lead time until changes are happening without notice.

Also: Lateness, Trying New Things, Uncertainty, Unfairness

C

CHARACTERS
See: Baddies, Costumed Characters

CHEATING
See: Losing, Mistakes

CHECKING
Considerations
This section relates to compulsive checking behaviors such as those seen in OCD, when a child feels compelled to check household appliances, light switches, or faucets to make sure they are off. They might also check windows and doors to make sure they are locked. Exposure focuses on the possibility that an appliance might be left on or a door unlocked while moving the child away from safety behaviors such as checking and reassurance-seeking.

Exposures

O Check less on purpose.
   Help the child become aware of checking, then challenge them to systematically decrease the number of checks they do until reaching zero.

O Use a **Token System** to keep track of checking questions.
   Start with three tokens a day. When a checking question is asked, the parent is to say, "That would be a token." The child then has a choice, they can give up a token to have the parent answer the question or say, "Never mind" and keep the token but get no answer. Unused tokens turn into points that can be cashed in for rewards. If the child uses all three tokens, then asks a fourth checking question, the parent is to say, "I'm sorry, you're out of tokens," and then not answer the question. The use of physical tokens is important as it interrupts the automaticity of asking and answering checking questions. Decrease the number of tokens available to the child over time.

O Use a playful sound to help you notice checking questions.
   Coach the parent to make a playful buzzing noise rather than answering checking questions. Another option would be to create a code word to signify checking questions. The goal of this exposure is to increase the child's awareness of checking questions while helping parents move away from routinely answering. Teach parents to buzz in a good-humored manner, remembering that they are aligned with their child as they learn to respond differently to anxiety.

C

○ Watch a parent use something that makes you want to check.
   Have the parent purposely and with notice engage in an activity that typically triggers checking, such as closing a window or using an appliance. Challenge the child to go about their business without checking or being reassured.

○ Let a parent use something that makes you want to check without watching them.
   Have the parent use a triggering item out of view of the child. The child must know the triggering item is being used, but does not come in to check and is not given reassurance.

○ Use something that makes you want to check.
   Have the child use a triggering item. Reduce and then eliminate checking. Once the child is able to use the item without checking, have them say a feared thought such as, "I may have left the light on," or "I may not have closed the door all the way." If the statement triggers checking or reassurance-seeking, systematically decrease, then eliminate, both.

○ Purposely do things your worry tells you might happen.
   Help the child become aware of feared outcomes connected to checking, such as wasting water by leaving a sink dripping, or ruining markers by leaving the caps off. Then, within the bounds of safety, have the child do these things on purpose.

Also: Intrusive Thoughts, Just Right Feeling, Re-Reading, Uncertainty

CHOICES
See: Making Decisions, Perfectionism, Social Anxiety, Uncertainty

CHOKING
Considerations
It is important to first make sure there is no substantive cause for a fear of choking such as a physical problem that makes swallowing difficult. Children with oral-motor planning challenges or oral sensory differences would be better served by a Speech and Language Pathologist or an Occupational Therapist, rather than using exposure. Additionally, children with thyroid dysfunction can feel like there is a lump in their throat and have trouble swallowing. Children with a fear of choking should be evaluated by their Primary Care Provider (PCP) to rule out medical issues prior to initiating exposure.

C

In the absence of physical causes, the fear of choking can arise from past experience, such as swallowing food wrong, or it can be a symptom of OCD or Pediatric Autoimmune Neuropsychiatric Disorders Associated with Streptococcal Infections (PANDAS/PANS). In these cases, it is appropriate to treat with ERP. Start by making a list of foods the child is avoiding. Ask the child to sort the list into three categories: foods that seem easy, medium, and hard to eat. Start with foods in the easiest category. Monitor for safety behaviors such as tiny bites, over-chewing, drinking after every bite, or eating only in the presence of others.

Some of the suggested exposures include eating at an unusual rate. While potentially concerning to parents, once the fear is resolved, the vast majority of children return to functional eating.

Exposures

○ Say the word *choke*.
Have the child say *choke* fast and slow, in different tones of voice or accents.

○ Write the word *choke*.
Have the child write the word *choke* in print, cursive, or bubble letters and color it in.

○ Draw a picture of a person choking.

○ Listen to choking sounds.
Begin with a brief choking sound at low volume. Gradually increase both the length and volume of the audio. Eventually make the challenge harder by having the child listen while eating.

○ Watch a movie that involves choking.
Prescreen to ensure that the movie is appropriate for children and that the choking scene ends well. It might be necessary to present the movie slowly, having the child watch just a portion to start, freezing the frame when the choking begins, or adding humor by watching backward or in slow motion to habituate the child to the scenes they find scary.

○ Take different-sized bites of food.
Challenge the child to take tiny bites, medium bites, and big bites of foods they routinely eat before moving to foods they avoid.

○ Drink less while eating.
Help the child reduce over-drinking by spreading sips out to every other bite,

C

every three bites, and so on. When drinking is used to mitigate the fear of choking, work toward eating without drinking at all.

○ Chew less.
Start with the child's baseline number of chews, then ask them to consciously chew less, systematically decreasing the number. You can also use a die to determine the number of chews, introducing the element of chance.

○ Eat alone.
Children who are afraid of choking often refuse to eat alone. Move from having the parent at the table, to across the room, to in another room, to out of the home entirely.

○ Eat a scary food.
Introduce the feared food by putting it on the child's plate. Over subsequent exposures, have the child move from tolerating the food on the plate, to taking a tiny bite, to a medium-sized bite that is chewed and spit out, to a medium bite that is chewed and swallowed.

○ Tell yourself you might choke while you are eating.
Once the child has resumed eating foods they've been avoiding, help them add the feared thought by saying, "I could choke on this," initially before eating, then while eating.

○ Play **Now!**
During meal- or snack-time, a designated person periodically calls out, "Now!," setting off 10 seconds of speed-eating for everyone at the table. Ham it up, turning this into a whacky mock competition.

○ Play **Beat the Clock** or **Beat the Parent**.
Challenge the child to eat a snack or part of a meal within a certain time or faster than their parent.

○ Play **Fewest Bites Wins**.
Using a variety of foods, including foods the child is and is not currently eating, compete to see who can eat each food with the fewest bites, *not chews but bites*.

○ Have a **Pretend Choking Contest**.
Make some rounds funny, such as "Who can act out the fastest choke?" and some more serious, such as "Who can act out the most realistic choke?"

C

○ Make yourself gag on purpose.
Begin where the child is comfortable. Progress from having the child lightly touch a tongue depressor to the front of their tongue to gradually, over subsequent exposures, moving it toward the back of their mouth until they are able to induce a gag. Begin by having an adult present before challenging the child to induce gagging alone. This exposure will be harder if done before or after eating.

○ Take a first aid for kids class.
Find a class that includes what to do if someone chokes.

Also: Panic, Selective Eating, Vomiting, Words and Phrases

CIGARETTES
See: Contamination, Drugs

CITIES
See: Confined Spaces, Crowded Places, Differentness, Heights, Noises, Separation Anxiety

CLOTHING
See: Buttons, Contamination

CLOWNS
See: Baddies, Costumed Characters

CONFINED SPACES
Considerations
There are two main concerns when it comes to the fear of confined spaces: getting stuck and feeling boxed in. While the former is more common, it is best to assess the focus of the child's fear prior to plunging in. Has the child had a frightening experience, such as not being able to open the door of a toilet stall, or getting stuck in a closet? If the child has experienced trauma in a confined space, Eye Movement Desensitization and Reprocessing (EMDR) or another trauma-informed technique can pave the way for exposure therapy.

C

Exposures

○ Look at pictures of small tight spaces.
Find pictures of feared spaces such as bathroom stalls or elevators. Move from images of a single, calm person in the space to multiple people crowded in.

○ Make yourself into a "burrito."
Gauge what the child is able to tolerate by first covering their body with a heavy blanket, then move to making a tighter roll, eventually encasing the child's whole body.

○ Climb into a sleeping bag head first.
Add challenges such as rolling over, lifting arms over head, or turning around in the bag to induce a trapped feeling.

○ Watch videos of people in small tight spaces.

○ Visit a small tight space.
Have the child start by standing outside the enclosed space with a support person. Over subsequent visits, have them move to the doorway, enter, and close the door, all accompanied by the support person. The challenge can be made more difficult by staying in the confined space for longer stretches of time. Follow this sequence again with the child doing each step alone.

○ Ride elevators.
Move from large to small or from glass to opaque walls. Have the child ride the elevators first with a support person and then, if the child is old enough, alone.

○ Say, "I'm trapped and I can't get out."
Initially have the child say this in an open room with a support person present. Then have them say it with their eyes closed, picturing the confined space. Move to having the child say, "I'm trapped" while standing in a confined space, first with an adult present, then alone.

Also: Choking, Crowded Places, Dizziness, Panic, Separation Anxiety, Vomiting

CONTAMINATION
Considerations
Children with contamination fears studiously avoid objects they see as poisonous, germy, or otherwise harmful. Of course, some things children encounter really are dangerous, for example insecticides, or visibly filthy public toilets.

C

Other items require caution, such as cleaning supplies and cigarette butts. And finally, there are everyday items that are safe but get associated with danger, like the shirt a child was wearing the last time they threw up. Exposure is used for incapacitating fear of items in the last two categories, those that are scary-seeming but safe and those that are safe when used with caution.

When doing exposure for objects the child sees as contaminated, pay attention to safety behaviors such as using a barrier to touch the object or immediately washing hands. A graduated approach would start with exposure to the "contaminated" object, followed by delaying safety behaviors, and then completely eliminating them.

Exposures

○ Be in the same room with the "contaminated" object.
Start with the object in the room but out of sight. Over subsequent exposures, bring it into sight, then have the child move closer to it until they are able to touch it.

○ Watch someone touch the thing that seems dangerous.
Have a support person touch the "contaminated" object, then have the child move closer to that person, and eventually touch them. The final stage would be having the child touch the "contaminated" person's hand.

○ Draw the "contaminated" object.
The goal of this exposure is for the child to tolerate being around the object for longer stretches of time, so ask the child to draw using the "contaminated" object as a model.

○ Touch the "contaminated" thing.
Have the child touch quickly at first, then in a more prolonged way.

○ Play **Find It**, taking turns hiding and finding the "contaminated" object.

○ Carry the "contaminated" object from one place to another.

○ Use the "contaminated" thing.
Have the child use the object in its intended way. For example, use a spray cleaner to clean something, hold a hand rail, or wear a shirt that seems unsafe.

○ Touch the "contaminated" thing, then touch other things.
Have the child touch the object and then intentionally spread the "contamination" to the other hand, their face, around the home, or onto preferred objects.

○ Touch the "contaminated" object, then eat.
Within the bounds of safety, have the child touch the "contaminated" object, then eat with the same hand without washing.

CLOTHING

○ Carry the "contaminated" clothing in your backpack.

○ Hang the "contaminated" clothing where you can see it.
Have the child hang the "contaminated" clothing first in a common area, then in their room. Move from having the clothing simply visible to wrapping it around or spreading it over things the child uses such as toys, favorite stuffed animals, and their bed.

○ Play with the clothing you usually avoid.
Roll the "contaminated" clothing into a ball and play **Catch** with it. Take turns tucking it into waistbands to play **Steal-the-Shirt**. Stuff it to make a life-size doll. Play **Hide and Seek** with it.

○ Wear clothing that seems dangerous.
Move from having the child put the clothing on and immediately take it off again to putting it on and leaving it for increasingly long stretches of time. You can make this into a game by adding a timer, or putting the clothing on inside out, backward, or upside down.

FOOD

○ Eat a **Dirty Dessert**.
This exposure is specific to children concerned about dirt, who can be encouraged to make and eat brown pudding with brown cookies crumbled on top, accessorized with gummy worms or candy mushrooms while talking about dirt.

○ Let someone touch your silverware.
Vary how much contact the other person has with the silverware, from a quick touch, to holding the handle, to touching the eating end. You can also vary who is doing the touching.

○ Eat food someone else has touched.
Vary how much contact the person has with the food, and who is doing the touching.

C

○ Share food.
Move toward using the same plate while eating finger-foods, or reaching in and eating out of the same bag.

○ Play **Guess What!**
Work with the child to make three lists: foods you already eat, foods you find hard to eat, and "No way!" foods. Using a blindfold, have the child taste foods from the first two lists, trying to see if they can guess what they are. As the child becomes more accustomed to foods on the second list, talk about incorporating the third list.

○ Eat food on its "Use by" date.
Using adult judgment, have the child knowingly eat food on its "Use by" date, then slightly past the date.

○ Stop checking expiration dates.
Have the parent use a thick marker to cross out expiration dates on food so they can't be checked.

○ Eat food that isn't perfect.
Serve the child food with imperfections such as a cracker with a black fleck or an apple with a small bruise. Have the child move from rejecting the food, to eating around the imperfection, to eating the food in its entirety. Increase the size of the imperfection over time.

○ Touch the ground before eating.
Have the child touch the ground before eating, without washing. Allow them to first eat with silverware, moving toward eating with the hand that touched the ground.

○ Eat something that has fallen on the floor.

FURNITURE

○ Lean against the furniture.

○ Sit on the furniture.
Begin by having the child briefly touch down on and spring back up from the furniture before moving to prolonged sitting. Over time, have them move closer to and eventually right onto the "contaminated" spot. If necessary, start with a barrier such as a sheet.

○ Make a fort out of the furniture.

- ○ Play **Simon Says, Follow the Leader**, or **Musical Chairs**.
  Each of these games requires the child to touch and sit on "contaminated" furniture repeatedly and for varying lengths of time.

- ○ Lie on the furniture.
  Move from having the child lie first on their back, then their side, then their belly. End by having them rub their face on the furniture, including the "contaminated" spot.

Also: Health, Intrusive Thoughts, Selective Eating, "Unhealthy" Foods, Uncertainty, Wiping

COSTUMED CHARACTERS

Considerations

This set of exposures is for children who are afraid of characters other people see as benign: sports mascots, clowns, storybook characters, and even Santa. Sometimes the fear centers on one particular character or mascot; sometimes it is generalized to all costumed characters. Fearful avoidance can seriously limit the child and family's life, with the child refusing to go to sporting events, the circus, theme parks, and into stores around the holidays.

Before starting exposure therapy, make a list of characters the child avoids, and have the child order it from the least to the most scary. Start with the least scary character, even if it is one the child rarely encounters.

For children afraid of characters most people see as malevolent, see Baddies.

Exposures

- ○ Say the name of the character.
  Have the child play with the name; say it fast and slow, in different tones of voice or accents.

- ○ Write the name of the character.
  Have the child write the name in print, cursive, or bubble letters and color it in.

- ○ Make an **Acrostic** of the character's name.
  Have the child write the name of the character vertically on a page, then write an adjective describing the character starting with each letter.

- ○ Make up a song, poem, limerick, haiku, or rhyme about the character.

C

○ Look at pictures of the character.
Start with drawings or cartoons and move toward photos or other realistic images.

○ Draw the character.

○ Write a story about the character.

○ Make a stop-motion animation about the character.

○ Decorate a picture of the character.
Print pictures of the character. Encourage the child to draw on them, adding clothing, hats, and scenes.

○ Do a puzzle of the character.
Find a puzzle or make one by printing an image of the character and cutting it into puzzle shapes for the child to assemble.

○ Hang up pictures of the character.

○ Use a picture of the character as a device screensaver or wallpaper.

○ Buy or make a toy character.
Using supplies such as clay, paper mache, or cloth, help the child make a replica of the character. Challenge them to play with it or display it somewhere.

○ Watch videos of the character.

○ Think about the character on purpose.
Have the child say the name of the character, write it, look at a picture, or draw it, initially with a support person and then alone in a room. Gradually increase the time between completing the character challenge and returning to an adult.

○ Pretend to be the character.
Start with activities that are not related to the character's role. Challenge the child to act out ordering a sandwich, getting up in the morning, or getting stuck on a math problem, all while pretending to be the character. Eventually playact activities for which the character is known.

○ Look for the character in a party or costume store.
The first visit might be limited to sitting in the parking lot. Over subsequent exposures, have the child move to the doorway of the store, and eventually walk in. Approach the images of the character on party goods. If there are

C

costumes of the character, touch them or try them on. Take a selfie with a life-size cut-out of the character.

○ Dress up like the character.

○ Visit the character in real life.
Visit a place known for having costumed characters, such as a sporting event, the mall around a holiday, or a children's entertainment venue. Start at a comfortable distance, and move toward approaching the character and eventually interacting with them. You can also contact a local athletic director, the fire department, or an entertainment venue for one-on-one access to a costumed character. Move from having the child view the character from afar to meeting it, both in and out of costume.

Also: Baddies, Navigating Home Alone, Sleeping Alone, Words and Phrases

CROWDED PLACES
Considerations
Sometimes children are avoidant or afraid of crowded places due to sensory processing concerns, which make these places too loud or visually taxing. Children can also have difficulty with vestibular processing, and may not trust their ability to not trip or bump into someone. After reasons such as these are ruled out or addressed, the fear of crowded spaces can be treated with exposure.

Exposures

○ Imagine crowds.
Tell stories involving large venues, describing the crowding in detail.

○ Watch videos of crowds.
Prescreen videos of street fairs, sporting events, concerts, and other venues known for large crowds before presenting them to the child. Start with the sound off, increasing the volume over time.

○ Visit crowded places.
Have the child visit a crowded venue such as a sporting event, movie, or mall with a support person. Move from watching from the sidelines to entering the crowd. Gradually decrease proximity to the support person, moving from holding hands to walking next to but not touching them. On subsequent visits, have the child walk further away from the support person.

C

○ Do something you enjoy in a crowded place.
Have the family go to a concert venue to see a musician the child likes, or go to a play or sporting event.

○ Do a **Scavenger Hunt** in a crowded place.
Items might include: a brown shoe, something red, a purse, a cane, a backpack, or a hat.

○ Sit in less comfortable places.
In a theater or on public transit, have the child move from sitting right next to a support person with body contact to sitting next to the support person without touching them. Eventually sit further apart. Sit in various spots, such as toward the front of a theatre or in the middle of a row.

Also: Confined Spaces, Dizziness, Panic, Separation Anxiety

C

D

DANGEROUS ANIMALS

Considerations

We want children to maintain a healthy awareness around animals that are truly dangerous. Exposure is used when a child's fear far outstrips the likelihood of harm, when there are no poisonous snakes in the region, for example, or when the child refuses to go to the beach even though shark sightings are rare. Remember that exposure never puts a child in actual danger. We are, instead, exposing the child to thinking about the feared animal, and to a reasonable level of risk.

Exposures

○ Say the name of the animal.
  Have the child play with the animal's name, saying it fast and slow, in different tones of voice or accents.

○ Write the name of the animal.
  Have the child use print, cursive, or bubble letters to make a word poster.

○ Find the animal in a **Hidden Picture**.

○ Do an animal **Word Search**.
  There are websites that will create a Word Search for you from relevant keywords. For the fear of sharks, words might include: shark, swim, ocean, eat, fish, teeth, fins, and surfing.

○ Draw the animal.

○ Look at pictures of the animal.
  Move from cartoon drawings to photos, and from far away to close up.

○ Decorate the animal.
  Print pictures of the animal. Have the child draw on them, adding clothing, hats, and scenes. Start with cartoonish, friendly images before moving to more realistic pictures.

○ Do an animal puzzle.
Find a puzzle or make one by printing an image of the animal and cutting it into puzzle shapes for the child to assemble.

○ Hang pictures of the animal.

○ Use a picture of the animal as a device screensaver or wallpaper.

○ Look at illustrated fact books about the animal.

○ Teach someone about the animal using pictures and facts.

○ Play **Catch** with the toy animal.

○ Play **Find It**, taking turns hiding and finding the toy animal.

○ Make animal arts and crafts.
Have the child create animal finger-puppets, pipe-cleaner animals, pasta animals, animal masks, or clay animals. Buy or make an animal cuddly toy.

○ Pretend to be the animal.
Play house, school, or living in the wild, incorporating the animal into the play.

○ Play **Gotcha!**
Take turns hiding plastic replicas, stuffed animals, or pictures of the feared animal. You might use plastic animals. When someone finds one, they get to re-hide it, which means that eventually the child will encounter the feared animal in unexpected places.

○ Go to a science museum, aquarium, or zoo to see the animal.
Have the child practice getting closer to the display, tank, or cage.

○ Do a **Scavenger Hunt**.
Visit a feared habitat, for example the woods for fear of snakes or the beach for fear of sharks. Make a list of things for the child to find while in that location. For a fear of snakes in the woods, the list could include: a leaf with four points, a feather, a heart-shaped rock, a fern, or a nest.

○ Do a **Color Card Scavenger Hunt**.
Visit the feared habitat and, using a paint-sample card, challenge the child to find those exact colors in nature.

D

○ Go on a **Photo Safari**.
Allow the child to take pictures in a feared habitat, challenging them to find various things. For example, a beach list might include: a seagull, a shell, an umbrella, a rock, seaweed, or pictures taken in the water.

Also: Bees, Snakes, Words and Phrases

DARK
Considerations
Fear of the dark is common among children, especially at certain developmental stages. Wanting to put the child at ease, parents often accommodate this fear, turning on extra lights, accompanying the child to darker parts of the home, or staying as the child falls asleep. Families often make their way into treatment when it becomes clear that accommodations are backfiring, by which time, fear of the dark is often firmly entrenched. The following exposures aim to habituate the child to being alone in the dark, helping them see that they are, in fact, safe. Often exposure to fear of the dark needs to be followed by exposures related to Navigating Home Alone and Sleeping Alone.

Exposures

○ Write a story about something that happens in the dark.

○ Watch a movie with nighttime scenes.
Look for children's movies, prescreening them to ensure that nothing dangerous happens in the dark.

○ Sit in a dark room or closet.
This exposure can be modified in a variety of ways including proximity to a support person, length of time in the room, and amount of distraction. You might have the child begin by sitting in the dark with a support person, moving that person further away over time until the child is sitting in the dark alone. Once they are sitting in the dark alone, allow the child to have a compelling distraction such as an audiobook. Fade out the distraction while increasing the length of time, eventually having the child sit in the dark with their imagination to occupy them for 15 or 20 minutes.

○ Walk to a dark area.
There are two parts to play with here, proximity to the parent and amount of light. As the child moves from turning on lights, to using a flashlight, to

D

leaving rooms dark, the parent can initially stand close by, talking the whole time. Over subsequent exposures, stop the talking, move the parent further away, slow down the pace of walking, and increase the length of time spent in the dark.

○ Play indoor **Nighttime Hide and Seek** using only flashlights.

○ Make shadow-puppets.
With the lights off, the parent or child can use a flashlight to make creatures on the wall. Have them create a story together and act it out using their shadow-puppets.

○ Play **Find It** in the dark.
Take turns hiding and finding a glow stick. Increase the play area over time so the entire home is eventually fair game.

○ Play **Nighttime Sardines**.
Move from semi-dark with nightlights, flashlights, or glow sticks to fully darkened rooms. When someone finds the person hiding, they join them until everyone is squeezed into the same space.

○ Go outside at night.
Begin by doing this with a bright porch light or flashlight, fading out the light over time. Increase the time spent outside. Include a support person if needed, increasing the distance between the child and support person over time.

○ Play **Flashlight Tag** or **Flashlight Hide and Seek** outside at night.

○ Do a **Reflector Hunt**.
Have the parent hang reflective tape or stickers inside or outside. Challenge the child to find all the reflectors using a flashlight.

Also: Baddies, Navigating Home Alone, Sleeping Alone

DEATH
Considerations
It is normal for children to be afraid of dying, and to get worried when they begin to understand that everyone, including their parents, will eventually die. Initial interventions include providing information, support, and reassurance. Exposure would only be used if the fear of death leads to the use of safety behaviors such as refusing to go upstairs alone, fall asleep alone, or eat certain foods.

D

Exposure would also be used for intrusive thoughts about death. If a child is grieving an actual death, or anticipating the death of a loved one who may die soon, supportive or trauma-informed techniques should be used instead.

See: Checking, Choking, Health, Intrusive Thoughts, Navigating Home Alone, Separation Anxiety, Sleeping Alone, Uncertainty, "Unhealthy" Foods

DECISIONS
See: Making Decisions, Uncertainty

DEFECATING
See: Toileting, Wiping

DENTISTS
Considerations
Anxiety about going to the dentist can arise when a child has had, or has heard about, an uncomfortable experience at a dental office. It can also occur without this history, when a child anticipates something painful occurring and clings to safety behaviors to protect themself.

When visiting a dental office as part of exposure therapy, an adult should call ahead and explain that the child is doing exposure to address their fear. Most dental offices have ample experience with fearful children, and they are typically happy to accommodate families addressing this fear.

Exposures

○ Say the dentist's name.
   Have the child play with the dentist's name, saying it fast and slow, in different tones of voice or accents.

○ Write the name of the dentist.
   Have the child write the name in print, cursive, or bubble letters and color it in.

○ Create a **Dental Guidebook**.
   Work with the child to take pictures of the parking lot, building from the outside, waiting room, reception area, and a treatment room, or find them online. Have the child help put together a book with captions. Read it periodically.

D

○ Draw yourself at the dentist's office.
Have the child draw a picture of themselves at the dentist's office. They could also draw onto photos of the office, or photoshop themself in. Hang the pictures around the home.

○ Play with a pretend dental kit.
Take turns as dentist and patient. Practice feared activities such as cleaning teeth, flossing, taking x-rays, or filling a cavity.

○ Watch videos taken in a dentist's office.
Prescreen videos taken in a dental office. Have the child listen without video, or watch with the sound muted, before combining video and audio. Make sure the videos include activities such as waiting in the waiting room, having teeth counted and cleaned, rinsing, and suction.

○ Imagine a dental visit.
Do an imaginal exposure with an adult narrating each step of a dental visit.

○ Go to a dentist's office.
First, have the child habituate to sitting in the parking lot with no intention of going in. Move to walking to the office door, still without an actual appointment, and then returning to the car. Over subsequent exposures, have the child enter the office and greet the receptionist. Gradually add waiting in the waiting room, saying hello to the dentist, watching someone else have a procedure done, and finally, sitting in the chair so the dentist can count the child's teeth.

○ Go for a full dental visit.

Also: Doctors, Injections, Words and Phrases

DIFFERENTNESS
Considerations
Children sometimes perceive differentness as dangerous, and begin to avoid or actively fear people with disabilities, older adults, teenagers, or people who look or sound different from them. It is helpful to not only normalize but also celebrate differences, and to make an effort to expose children to books, movies, and people who are different from them. Parents can model interest in and acceptance of a full range of people, neither accommodating their child's fear nor shaming them for it.

D

Exposures

○ Read a book about a person who seems different from the child.

○ Look at photos of people who seem different.
Focusing on the differences that make the child nervous, look for images that show people doing a variety of things, including activities familiar or of interest to the child.

○ Learn about organizations related to the feared difference.
Help the child do research into organizations involving people with the feared characteristic. If possible, facilitate a volunteer experience such as handing out fliers, delivering cookies, talking to residents, or helping in some other way.

○ Watch a movie with a character who seems different.
Prescreen movies for age-appropriateness and benefit to the child. Once a movie has been selected, talk about it with the child and look at still images. Move to watching a trailer for the movie, then a portion of the movie. Over subsequent exposures, watch the entire movie. Although this is an exposure activity, it can be paired with reframing to show how all people are different from one another in some ways and the same in other ways.

○ Watch real-life videos of people who seem different.
Prescreen the videos, then present them in order from easier-seeming to more challenging, depending on the focus of the child's fear.

○ Meet and spend time with someone who seems different.

Also: Crowded Places

DIRT/DIRTY
See: Contamination

DISABILITY
See: Differentness, Health

D

DIVORCE

Considerations

It is not unusual for children to wonder if their parents will get a divorce. If parents are, in fact, in conflict, intervention would begin with information and support. Exposure would only be used if there is no indication that the marriage is in trouble and yet the child's fear of divorce leads to safety behaviors such as excessive reassurance-seeking, always having to be with a parent, difficulty falling asleep alone, or school refusal. In these cases, exposure would be to the activities or situations the child is avoiding. Exposure would also be used for intrusive thoughts about divorce, especially when the thoughts cause significant distress or make it difficult to participate in school, hobbies, or family life.

See: Intrusive Thoughts, Navigating Home Alone, Separation Anxiety, Sleeping Alone, Uncertainty, Words and Phrases

DIZZINESS

Considerations

The fear of dizziness often occurs alongside apprehension about fainting, vomiting, and panic. Once medical causes have been ruled out, exposure focuses on activities that result in dizziness. This helps the child feel less frightened by what is admittedly a disconcerting feeling, and tolerate it long enough to have the dizziness fade on its own.

Exposures

○ Spend time in a big room.
  Find a high-ceilinged room, or return to a room in which the child has felt dizzy in the past. Gradually lengthen the time spent in the room, and challenge the child to do things likely to induce dizziness, such as spinning or looking up.

○ Make yourself dizzy by sitting with your head between your knees for 30 seconds.

○ Make yourself dizzy by spinning around on a desk chair or tire swing.
  Also try a playground merry-go-round or holding hands, leaning back, and spinning. Work with the speed and amount of spin-time to find the right level of exposure, increasing both over time.

D

○ Make yourself dizzy with breathing.
Have the child breathe through a straw or heavily into a paper bag to pur-posely induce dizziness, watching an adult do each of these things first. The aim is to safely demystify dizziness, and even to play with it, so the child learns that dizziness is uncomfortable but not dangerous.

○ Make yourself dizzy by turning your head back and forth gently for 30 sec-onds, as if saying "No."

○ Have a **Pretend Fainting Contest**.
See who can act out fainting most dramatically. Vary the scenarios to include pretending to faint in feared locations.

Also: Panic, Vomiting

DOCTORS
Considerations
Anxiety about doctors can arise when a child has had, or has heard about, an uncomfortable experience with a doctor. It can also happen when the child anticipates something painful occurring and clings to safety behaviors to protect themselves.

When visiting a doctor's office as part of exposure therapy, an adult should call ahead and explain that the child is doing exposure to address their fear. Most medical offices have ample experience with fearful children, and they are typically happy to accommodate families addressing this fear.

Exposures

○ Say the doctor's name.
Have the child play with the doctor's name, saying it fast and slow, in differ-ent tones of voice or accents.

○ Write the name of the doctor.
Have the child write the name in print, cursive, or bubble letters and color it in.

○ Create a **Doctor's Office Guidebook**.
Work with the child to take pictures of the parking lot, building from the outside, waiting room, reception area, and a treatment room, or find them online. Have the child help put together a book with captions. Read it periodically.

D

○ Draw yourself at the doctor's office.
Have the child draw a picture of themselves at the doctor's office. They could also draw onto photos of the office, or photoshop themself in. Hang the pictures around the home.

○ Play with a toy doctor's kit.
Take turns as doctor, nurse, and patient. Practice feared activities such as taking blood pressure and looking into ears and mouth.

○ Watch videos taken in a doctor's office.
Prescreen videos taken in a medical office. Have the child listen to the sounds alone, or watch with the sound muted, before combining video and audio. Make sure the videos include activities such as waiting in the waiting room, getting weighed and measured, having blood pressure taken, and talking to the doctor.

○ Imagine a visit to the doctor.
Do an imaginal exposure with an adult narrating each step a medical visit.

○ Go to a doctor's office.
Have the child first habituate to sitting in the parking lot with no intention of going in. Move to walking to the office door, still without an actual appointment, and then returning to the car. Over subsequent exposures, have the child enter the office and greet the receptionist. Gradually add waiting in the waiting room, saying hello to the nurse or doctor, watching someone else have a procedure done, and finally, doing something easy like getting weighed or measured. Have the child take a selfie with the doctor.

○ Go for a full medical visit.

Also: Blood, Dentists, Health, Injections, Words and Phrases

DOGS
Considerations
We struggled with what to call this category as the exposures listed here are applicable to any household pet. But the reality is that the fear of dogs is substantially more common than the fear of cats, hamsters, or rabbits. If you are treating a child afraid of a pet other than a dog, feel free to substitute the relevant animal.

Please keep in mind that we want children to understand and follow basic safety rules around dogs, especially those not known to the family. Teach the

D

dog-phobic child how to read behavioral cues including tail placement, barking, and sniffing. Explain that dogs calm down when the humans around them are calm. Allow the child to watch this in action, either with real-life dogs or online. When doing exposures, it is best to start with sedentary animals. Anxious children and anxious dogs are never a good mix.

The goal with children who are afraid of dogs is to acclimate to dogs as a category rather than to one particular animal. Move from familiar to unfamiliar dogs, from small to larger dogs, and from sedentary to more active dogs. When doing exposures with unfamiliar dogs, use appropriate caution, beginning with a conversation with the dog owner about the dog's temperament and what you would like to do.

Exposures

- ○ Look at pictures of dogs.
  Begin with cartoon drawings, then move to more realistic drawings and photos.

- ○ Draw dogs.
  Move from having the child draw from memory to drawing while looking at photos and eventually viewing dogs from afar while drawing them.

- ○ Buy or make a stuffed dog toy.
  Move from keeping the toy in a drawer or otherwise out of view to naming it, playing with it, and eventually sleeping with it.

- ○ Read books with dog characters.

- ○ Read fact books to learn about dogs.

- ○ Play the **Alphabet Game** with dog breeds.
  For example: A-Afghan Hound, B-Beagle, C-Collie, D-Dachshund…

- ○ Use dog pictures as device wallpaper or screensavers.

- ○ Listen to dog sounds.
  Find audio of dogs barking, panting, and making other typical noises. Start by doing an activity while the sound plays at low volume in the background, then move to listening at full volume and without distraction.

- ○ Watch videos of dogs.
  Move from smaller to larger, and sedentary to active animals. Watch videos that include feared activities such as barking or jumping. Do not, however, include videos of dogs attacking or biting people.

D

○ Take a field trip to watch dogs.
Bring the child to local venues where they are likely to see dogs. Have the child watch from afar before challenging them to gradually move closer.

○ Take a walk, counting the dogs you see.

○ Do a **Dog Scavenger Hunt** or play **Dog Bingo.**
Find: a tall dog, a short dog, a fat dog, a dog wearing something colorful, a dog that is: eating, sleeping, sniffing, barking, or running.

Dog Bingo

B	I	N	G	O
Short dog	Running dog	Fancy collar	Spotted dog	Floppy ears
Pointy ears	Leashed dog	Barking dog	Sniffing dog	Wagging tail
Curly fur	Puppy	★	Service dog	Black dog
Pair of dogs	Dog in a coat	Sleeping dog	Drinking dog	Happy dog
Tiny dog	Brown dog	Jumping dog	Dog toy	Eating dog

○ Stand out of reach of a dog on a leash.
Move closer over time.

○ Go to a pet store or place where dogs get groomed.
Have the child watch dogs coming and going from inside the car, then from the doorway. Eventually walk with the child through the aisles of the store. Watch a dog being groomed.

○ Visit a friend or relative who owns a dog.
Begin by having the dog closed off in another room during the visit. Then visit with the dog in the same room, but on a leash. Move to being in a room with the dog off-leash and, finally, playing with it.

○ Stand near a sleeping dog that is not on a leash.

○ Let a dog you know sniff your hand.
Start with the dog on a leash. Over subsequent exposures, move to the same dog off-leash. Visit other dogs known to the family, varying the age, size, and activity level of the dog.

D

- ○ Pet a dog that you or your parents know.
  Start with the dog on a leash, moving to off-leash over subsequent exposures. Pet other known dogs, varying the age, size, and activity level of the dog.

- ○ Feed a dog a treat.
  Have the child move from putting the treat on the ground in front of the dog to feeding it by hand.

- ○ Stay near a dog you know that is not on a leash.
  Have the child do this activity outdoors, moving from watching the dog off-leash to interacting with it by throwing a stick or ball, or petting it.

- ○ Visit an animal rescue center or shelter.

Also: Pet Escaping

DOLLS
Considerations
The fear of dolls often centers on the possibility of the doll coming to life, especially at night. Sometimes children have heard stories featuring living dolls, and sometimes they have imagined this themselves. Often it is the creepiness of the doll's eyes that is problematic, leading to safety behaviors such as reassurance-seeking, avoiding dolls, or consistently turning them away.

Exposures

- ○ Look at pictures of dolls.

- ○ Read a book about a doll.

- ○ Use a picture of a doll as a device screensaver or wallpaper.

- ○ Make your own doll.
  Using craft supplies, have the child make their own doll.

- ○ Be in the same room as a doll.
  Decrease the distance from the doll over time. Add an activity such as reading to the doll, dressing it, having a tea party, or otherwise playing with it.

- ○ Play **Find It**, taking turns hiding and finding a doll.

- ○ Play **Catch** with a doll.

- ○ Carry a doll around in a backpack.

D

○ Sleep with a doll in the room.
Start with the doll across the room, moving it toward the bed, and ultimately into the bed. If the child is especially afraid of the doll's eyes, move from having the doll face a wall to having it face the child.

Also: Baddies, Navigating Home Alone

DOWNSTAIRS
See: Navigating Home Alone

DRUGS
Considerations
This category refers to the fear of drugs, alcohol, cigarettes, or any ingestible product the child sees as illegal or harmful. Some children present with the fear that they accidentally ingested a substance, or that they might accidently ingest it. Some worry they will develop an addiction. The fear of drugs can interfere with the child's ability to walk on sidewalks, take needed medicines, or be around adults who are drinking.

The activities listed here do not expose children to second-hand smoke or illegal substances and they do not encourage alcohol consumption. The point of exposure is to support children to be able to function successfully in a world where substances exist.

Many of the exposures use prescription pills, supplements, or over-the-counter medications. While the adult doing the exposure will be monitoring for safety, the activities should be done without repeatedly reassuring the child.

Exposures
ALCOHOL

○ Say the name repeatedly, such as *beer, beer, beer*.

○ Look at pictures of people drinking.

○ Watch videos of people drinking.
Prescreen to find videos of people drinking but not getting drunk.

○ Stay in a room with an adult who is drinking.
The exposure is to drinking, not drunkenness, so be sure to coach parents accordingly. Have the child move from doing something like watching a show

D

together to having a thumb war. Difficulty can be notched up by having the child eat during or just after the activity, without washing hands.

○ Stand near a bottle of alcohol.
Begin with an empty, clean bottle, then a full, capped bottle, and finally an open bottle with alcohol in it. Move from standing near the bottle to touching it.

○ Do an alcohol label **Scavenger Hunt**.
Challenge the child to find: the prettiest label, the funniest label, a label with an animal on it, or a label with a word they don't know. Have the child touch the bottles.

○ Use an empty alcohol bottle in an art project.

○ Drink out of a glass that is used for alcohol.
Find glasses the child associates with alcohol such as a beer mug, wine glass, or shot glass. Have the child routinely drink water, milk, or juice from these glasses. Remind parents to not provide reassurance during this exposure.

○ Play **Guess the Smell**.
Blindfold the child and have them identify liquids, including alcohol, by smell alone. Be sure to include familiar liquids such as milk, lemonade, a favorite soft drink, water, or tea, along with one or two kinds of alcohol. Take turns as the "sniffer," with the child preparing secret cups for the adult to smell, as handling alcohol bottles and pouring from them is an exposure, too.

○ Have a **Relay Race** with alcohol.
Move alcohol a spoonful at a time from the starting line to a small cup several feet away. Whoever fills their cup first wins!

○ Create alcohol arts and crafts.
Finger paint with alcohol. Make a mobile out of wine corks or a picture out of beer caps.

○ Dip your finger into a glass of alcohol.
Move from immediately wiping the alcohol off to having the child rub it into their hand like lotion. This exposure can be made more challenging by then eating with the hand that touched the alcohol. The child may need to first nibble around the parts of the food they are touching before eating the food in its entirety.

D

CIGARETTES

○ Say *cigarettes* repeatedly.
Play with the word saying it fast, slow, with accents, and many times fast.

○ Look at pictures of cigarettes and cigarette butts.

○ Look at pictures of people smoking.

○ Watch videos of smokers.

○ Take a walk, looking for cigarette butts.
Over subsequent walks, have the child move closer to the butts and eventually touch them with a stick or nudge them with the toe of their shoe. Watch for avoidance of that shoe afterward, and fade out safety behaviors. Exposure to the "contaminated" shoe may be necessary.

○ Play **Catch** with a package of cigarettes.

○ Play **Find It**, taking turns hiding and finding a package of cigarettes.

○ Touch an unsmoked cigarette.
Move from quickly touching the cigarette to sustained contact by, for example, building a small house or campfire using cigarettes as logs. Initially allow the child to wash their hands after touching the cigarettes, then move to having them rub their arms, face, and eventually lips, all without washing.

○ Touch a cigarette and then eat something.

○ Carry a cigarette or butt.
Put a cigarette or butt in a zip lock bag and have the child carry it in their pocket, starting with a short period of time.

DRUGS

○ Say the name of the drug repeatedly.

○ Look at pictures of pills or other drugs.

○ Sit near a pill bottle or something else that reminds you of drugs.

○ Play **Hide the Pill Bottle**.

○ Play **Toss** with a pill bottle.
Use tiny crumpled balls of paper and see how many the child can toss into an empty pill bottle.

D

○ Use pill bottles for arts and crafts.
For example, draw eyes on pill bottles and use them as finger-puppets.

○ Make music with pill bottles.
Experiment by putting different items in pill bottles and listening to the sounds they make when shaken like maracas.

○ Use pill bottles to hold things like paper clips or hair ties.

○ Juggle pills.

○ Go fishing for candies.
Pour supplements or vitamins into a baggie. Mix in small candies that are distinctly different from the pills. Have the child "fish" for the candies by reaching into the bag, extracting the candies, and eating them.

Also: Contamination, Intrusive Thoughts, Words and Phrases

D

EARTHQUAKES
See: Weather

EATING
See: Choking, Contamination, Selective Eating, "Unhealthy" Foods, Vomiting

ELEVATORS
See: Confined Spaces, Escalators

EMBARRASSMENT
See: Mistakes, Perfectionism, Social Anxiety, Speaking

EMOTIONS
See: Feelings

ERRORS
See: Losing, Mistakes, Perfectionism

ESCALATORS
Considerations
For children who seldom ride escalators, there is something understandably disconcerting about stepping onto a moving staircase. Especially when coupled with sensory processing or visual tracking difficulty, it is easy to see why

escalators feel risky. Assess for these confounding variables prior to initiating exposure.

Unless you live in a city, it might be hard to find escalators to practice with. Think in terms of airports, malls, large office buildings, and public transit stations. As you begin exposure, remember that going up is typically easier than going down. Scope out elevators and staircases ahead of time so the child can practice riding up escalators repeatedly without needing to ride down before they are ready.

Exposures

○ Read a fact book about escalators.

○ Tell stories about escalators.
Take turns telling stories, or create a story together. Make some stories silly and some serious. Include mishaps and minor accidents.

○ Watch people riding escalators.

○ Send a toy up an escalator.

○ Act out stepping onto and off of an escalator.

○ Ride a moving walkway.
Have the child ride first with a support person, then alone.

○ Ride up an escalator.
Allow the child to hold hands with their support person to start, moving toward having the child step on first and stand in front of the support person. Also practice having the child step on second and ride behind the support person. Eventually have the child ride up alone.

○ Walk up an escalator.
Start with holding hands, then shift to having the child walk in front of or behind the support person and, finally, alone.

○ Ride down an escalator.
Allow the child to hold hands with their support person to start, moving toward having the child step on first and stand in front of the support person. Also practice having the child step on second and ride behind the support person. Eventually have the child ride down alone.

$\mathcal{E}$

○ Walk down an escalator.

Start with holding hands, then shift to having the child walk down in front of or behind the support person and, finally, alone.

○ Do a **Treasure Hunt** or **Scavenger Hunt**.

Bring the child to an appropriate venue, such as a mall with multiple escalators. Leave clues in envelopes for the child to find, leading to a prize at the end. Or have the child find items such as: a flashing sign, a place that sells food, something that smells good, or all the colors of the rainbow.

FAILURE

See: Losing, Mistakes, Perfectionism

FAINTING

See: Dizziness, Panic

FECES

See: Contamination, Toileting, Wiping

FEELINGS

Considerations

Some children find all expressions of emotion difficult, whereas others specifically avoid the emotions most people find uncomfortable, such as anger, sadness, or jealousy. Children who are feelings-averse often answer questions about feelings with, "I don't know." They may shut down when presented with activities or books about feelings, or angrily insist, "I'm fine!" when clearly they are not. Feelings-averse children may experience emotions as scary, or confusing, or both. For children with anxiety about feelings, exposure might occur alongside other interventions such as direct teaching about identifying feelings and self-regulation.

When a child has trouble tolerating strong feelings, it is important to monitor how the parent responds. Do they get angry, placate, or withdraw? If there is a pattern of trying to make big feelings go away, the parent may need coaching on self-regulation and co-regulation.

Exposures

O Play **Which One is Not Like the Others**?
Present sets of three pictures expressing the same feeling and a fourth showing a different feeling. Have the child identify which is different.

O Look at feelings pictures.
Show pictures of people expressing various emotions. Ask the child to name each feeling. Later, as feelings are expressed, have the child look at the pictures to identify what they are feeling.

O Draw about feelings.
Have the child draw what they are currently feeling, or how they felt during or about an event.

O Create an **All About Me** poster.
Help the child create a poster including items such as: I get mad when…, My happiest day was…, My family makes me feel…

O Play **Animal Feelings Charades**.
Put a list of feelings in one container and a list of animals in another. Each player picks a card from each container, then acts out the feeling as that animal. Take turns acting and guessing. Older children might want to play **Feelings Charades** without the animal component.

O Play **Guess the Feeling**.
Watch the child's preferred video content, prescreened. Periodically stop the video to ask, "What is that person feeling?" and "How can you tell?"

O Make a **Feelings Pie Chart**.
Draw a circle. Have the child choose a color for each of the four basic feelings: happy, mad, sad, and nervous. Ask the child to color in the pie chart showing how much of their day is filled by each feeling.

O Make a **Feelings Timeline**.
Draw a long rectangle with the child's activities for the day written underneath. Using different colors for happy, mad, sad, and

Feelings

Happy	Sorry
Sad	Grateful
Worried	Energetic
Mad	Bashful
Disappointed	Confused
Excited	Curious
Proud	Frustrated
Nervous	Eager
Silly	Generous
Friendly	Joyful
Content	Relaxed
Bored	Motivated
Embarrassed	Angry
Jealous	Tired
Remorseful	Surprised

F

nervous, have the child color the rectangle with the color representing the feeling they had during each activity. Some children may want to include additional feelings.

○ Reach into the **Feelings Jar**.
Create a Feelings Jar with slips of paper naming both enjoyable and uncomfortable feelings. Take turns drawing out a slip of paper, reading the feeling-word, and giving an example of a time you felt that way.

○ Play **Ding! Name That Feeling**.
Set a timer to go off at random intervals. When the timer sounds, everyone says what they are feeling.

○ Play **Roses and Thorns**.
Take turns identifying a high point and a low point of the day, as well as the associated feeling.

Also: Losing, Perfectionism, Social Anxiety, Unfairness

FIRE
Considerations
We want children to be cautious around fire, but when healthy apprehension turns to paralyzing fear, exposure becomes necessary. The goal is to have children understand and follow widely agreed upon safety rules without completely avoiding fireplaces, candles, grills, and the like. When fear arises following a fire-related trauma, treat the trauma first.

Exposures

○ Draw pictures of fires.

○ Make fire arts and crafts.

○ Look at pictures of fire.
Start with small flames on candles, then move to contained fireplace fires, and eventually campfires and larger blazes. Do not include pictures of fires burning out of control.

○ Look at videos of fires.
Move from flickering candles to fireplace fires, then campfires and larger blazes. Avoid raging wildfires and burning buildings. Difficulty can be adjusted by manipulating the sound and intensity of the videos.

F

- ○ Tell a story about fire.

- ○ Listen to a story about fire.
  Do an imaginal exposure with an adult describing the child appropriately interacting with fire.

- ○ Stand across the room from someone lighting a match.
  Have the child move closer over time.

- ○ Stand near a lit candle.
  Have the child move closer to the candle, and eventually hold it.

- ○ Stay in the kitchen when a gas stove is lit.
  Have the child move closer to the stove. Older children can eventually stir the contents of a pot on a lit burner.

- ○ Help build an outdoor fire.
  Work with the child to gather wood for an outdoor fire, such as in a fire pit. An adult should light the fire. Challenge the child to move closer and eventually stand next to the fire, first momentarily, then in a sustained way. Roasting marshmallows is likely to increase motivation.

FLAWS
See: Losing, Mistakes, Perfectionism, Social Anxiety, Trying New Things

FLOODS
See: Weather

FLYING
Considerations
Children pick up clues from people around them about whether or not an activity such as flying is safe. Therefore, if others in the family are afraid of flying, it would be best to address the fear collectively. If, on the other hand, the child has witnessed a stranger panicking on a flight, debrief with the child as quickly as possible, maintaining respect and compassion for the phobic person. Reminding children that we can be afraid of things that are not actually dangerous is a good place to start, as is teaching basic self-regulation skills.

Children sometimes develop a fear of flying after feeling uncomfortable on a previous flight. Having your ears pop, for example, feels odd and is sometimes

F

painful, and turbulence is disconcerting even to adults. Preparing the child for the sights, sounds, and sensations they are likely to experience helps, as does taking precautions, such as chewing gum, to keep the child comfortable. When a fear of flying makes it difficult for the family to travel, exposure can help.

Exposures

○ Make up a story about an imaginary trip involving flying and illustrate it.

○ Ask people about plane rides they've taken.
Have the child interview prescreened relatives and friends about airplane travel.

○ Listen to plane sounds.
Move from listening while doing an unrelated fun activity to listening without distraction.

○ Create a presentation with pictures and facts about planes.

○ Watch videos of planes.
Prescreen the videos to ensure they include getting a boarding pass, going through security, getting on the plane, taking off, flying, landing, and exiting the plane. Move to videos that show normal turbulence. The adult should narrate what is happening in the video, highlighting the helpers, the safety features, and various noises. Talk about the pilot and crew knowing where to go and what to do.

○ Listen to a story about flying.
Do an imaginal exposure narrating the process of going to the airport, going through security, getting on a plane, taking off, traveling, experiencing turbulence, landing, and exiting.

○ Visit an airport.
If the family lives near an airport, encourage frequent visits, starting with driving around the airport, then parking and going in. On subsequent visits, have the child watch take-offs and landings.

○ Use virtual reality and games to simulate flying.
Videos and games should be prescreened, with the amount of exposure carefully adjusted by the therapist.

○ Take a plane ride.
If possible, begin with a short trip to someplace fun.

Also: Confined Spaces, Intrusive Thoughts, Motion Sickness, Panic, Vomiting

F

FOOD
See: Choking, Contamination, Selective Eating, "Unhealthy" Foods

FROGS
Considerations
The fear of frogs is similar to other animal fears, often arising from an encounter that took the child by surprise and morphed into fear. Disgust is sometimes a factor, as well. For those who live in cities and suburbs, it's easy to avoid frogs, so many families let this fear go unaddressed. But when a child avoids outdoor settings because they might see a frog, it makes sense to do exposure. Any amphibian can be substituted in the exposures listed below.

Exposures

○ Say the word *frog*.
Have the child play with the word, saying it fast and slow, in different tones of voice or accents.

○ Write the word *frog*.
Have the child write the word in print, cursive, or bubble letters and color it in.

○ Make frog arts and crafts.
Have the child create frog finger-puppets, pipe-cleaner frogs, pasta frogs, frog masks, or clay frogs.

○ Play with toy frogs or pretend to be a frog.
Play house, school, or living in the wild.

○ Look at pictures of frogs.
Move from cartoon drawings to photos and from attractive to creepier-looking frogs.

○ Decorate pictures of frogs.
Have the child draw on pictures of frogs, adding clothing, hats, and scenes.

○ Do a frog puzzle.
Buy or make a puzzle by printing an image of a frog and cutting it into shapes for the child to assemble.

○ Hang frog art.

○ Use a picture of a frog as a device screensaver or wallpaper.

F

○ Learn about the frog life cycle.

○ Write a story about a frog.
Encourage the child to add details about the frog's life, friends, and ambitions.

○ Play **Catch** with toy frogs.

○ Play **Find It**, take turns hiding and finding a toy frog.

○ Play **Gotcha!**
Have the family take turns hiding toy frogs around the home. When some-one finds a frog, they get to re-hide it, which means that eventually the child will start encountering toy frogs in unexpected places. Realistic toy frogs will make this game more challenging.

○ Give a presentation about frogs with pictures and facts.

○ Listen to frog sounds.

○ Go to a science museum or zoo with an amphibian exhibit.
Have the child practice getting closer to the tanks.

○ Do a **Color Card Scavenger Hunt**.
Using green and brown paint samples, challenge the child to find those exact colors in nature, then frogs in those colors.

○ Do a **Scavenger Hunt**.
Make a list of things for the child to find in a place where frogs might live. For example: a bug, a flower, a rock, or an acorn.

○ Go on a **Frog Photo Safari**.
Have the child experiment with different angles and close-ups. If it is too difficult to find frogs, take pictures in nature, especially in spots where frogs could live. Edit frogs into the pictures.

○ Catch frogs, first with a net and then barehanded.

○ Get a pet frog to keep in a terrarium.
Have the child help with caretaking.

Also: Words and Phrases

FURNITURE
See: Contamination

F

GAGGING
See: Choking, Medicine (fear of swallowing), Vomiting

GERMS
See: Contamination, Intrusive Thoughts, Vomiting, Wiping

GETTING RID OF THINGS
Considerations
There are ordinary phases of childhood in which a child might collect things or be hesitant to throw them away. For example, a 5-year-old may fear their belongings would be sad if they were discarded. Or an 8-year-old might enjoy acquiring, organizing, and learning about a new passion. However, collecting behavior needs treatment when it becomes secretive, unsanitary, unsafe, or when it causes conflict in the family. For both general decluttering and specific exposure activities, coach parents to clean and sort with their child rather than secretly disposing of things. Daily and weekly routines for cleaning the child's room and common spaces will help with the accumulation of "stuff."

Exposures

○ Participate in family sort-outs.
Encourage the parent to create annual family traditions for thinning belongings. Birthdays, springtime, back to school, or the holiday season all offer annual opportunities to consider one's "stuff." Before buying new school clothes, for example, have the child try on old clothes and get rid of items

that no longer fit. During the holiday season, sort through and donate toys that are no longer used.

○ Clean one small area.
Begin with a single area such as a bookshelf, toy bin, or closet. Have the child sort everything in that one area into one of three categories: keep, put into storage, or give away. Set goals, such as an even number of items in each category, or having only X number of things in the keep pile. Items designated for storage should go into long-term storage, not readily available to the child. Incentivize putting things into the give away pile with a reward relevant to the child.

○ Follow the **One In, One Out** rule.
Teach the child that everything has a designated space. For example, clothing belongs in the dresser, books on the bookshelf, and toys in a bin. The confines of the space dictate how much of something will fit. So, when the designated space is full, follow the One In, One Out rule, getting a new item only after letting go of an old one.

○ Learn strategies for deciding what to keep.
Work with the child to develop guidelines about when to keep something and when to let it go. For example, clothing needs to fit, toys must have been played with in the past year, art projects need to fit on a particular shelf. If an item doesn't meet the criteria, it should go into long-term storage or leave the home.

○ Practice saying good-bye to things you are getting rid of.
Help the child create good-bye rituals such as a going-away party for old stuffed animals, a library visit for books being donated, or a marshmallow roast over school papers being burned. Taking photos of objects with senti-mental value also helps children let them go.

○ Decide what to keep by the numbers.
Have the child rate objects on a scale of 0–10, where 10 means "I really, really need to keep this" and 0 means "I don't use it and it isn't important to me." Encourage the child to use the full range of numbers. Start by getting rid of the 0s, 1s, and 2s, working up to the higher numbers over time.

Also: Growing Up

G

GHOSTS
See: Baddies, Dark, Navigating Home Alone

GOING UPSTAIRS OR DOWNSTAIRS ALONE
See: Navigating Home Alone

GROWING UP
Considerations
Many children talk about not wanting to grow up, particularly when they are staring down a developmental milestone like losing a tooth or going on their first sleepover. Some children are specifically afraid of puberty and the body changes involved. Growing up is associated with change, loss, responsibility, and uncertainty, which is why some children seek to avoid reminders that it is happening. While exposure to growing up happens naturally, the exposures listed below provide a more direct approach for children who are struggling.

Exposures

O   Talk about the things that are changing.
    Children who feel anxious about growing up often avoid talking about it. Rather than accommodating, engage the child in talking about changes, including how they are feeling and what aspects they want to preserve. For example, when a child learns that Santa isn't real, talk about how to hold onto what was special about Santa.

O   Make a list of things you can do now that you are older.

O   Talk to grown-ups about what it was like when they were your age.

O   Act out stories about people growing up.

O   Draw pictures of yourself at different ages.
    Prompt the child to draw a picture of themselves as a baby, their current age, a teenager, and then an older person.

O   Look at family photos.
    Reminisce while looking at family photos.

○ Plan your next birthday.
Help the child think ahead to their next birthday, considering venues or experiences available to them now that they are older.

○ Talk about the future.
Talk about what the child imagines for their teen years and adulthood. What will they be interested in? Where will they live? What kind of car will they drive? Will they have pets? What will they do all day?

○ Read books about older children.

Also: Getting Rid of Things, Intrusive Thoughts, Separation Anxiety, Uncertainty

G

HALLOWEEN
See: Baddies, Costumed Characters

HARM
See: Hurting Oneself or Others, Intrusive Thoughts

HEALTH
Considerations
Some children are overly concerned about their health, with fears that jump from Lyme Disease, to cancer, to heart attacks. Other children have more focused fears, such as stopping breathing in the night, or choking. Children with fears about health typically exhibit a combination of reassurance-seeking and avoidance. The goal of exposure is to reduce and ultimately eliminate these unnecessary behaviors while approaching whatever activities are being avoided, such as eating lunch at school or sleeping alone. Always work with the child's healthcare provider to rule out possible medical causes for the child's health-related anxiety before beginning exposure.

Exposures

○ Do a **Word Search** about your worries.
There are websites that will create a Word Search after you enter relevant keywords such as: fever, doctor, bump, rash, throw up, headache, woozy, or sore.

○ Go to the school nurse less often.
Move from the child going to the nurse on demand to going once or twice a day at scheduled times. Eventually give a limited number of nurse-passes for the child to use each week. Reward the child for unused visits.

○ Ask for fewer reassurances about your body.
Children often try to involve an adult in checking for symptoms, such as by feeling the child's forehead, taking their temperature, examining their tonsils, or palpating bumps. Use a Token System to gradually decrease the number of checks each day, offering rewards for unused tokens. Cover or remove mirrors and other objects used by the child to check themself. Teach parents to give neutral responses to the child's requests for reassurance. For example, "I have no reason to believe you have cancer," or "You might faint, and you might not. Let's wait and see what happens."

○ Read a story about a child who was sick and then got better.

○ Make yourself nauseous or dizzy on purpose.
Teach the child to induce, then tolerate, feared sensations. Over time, make the challenge more difficult by having the child say to themself, "It's always possible I'll throw up," or "I might faint" while inducing the physiological sensations.

Also: Choking, Dizziness, Panic, Sleeping Alone, Uncertainty, "Unhealthy" Foods, Vomiting

HEIGHTS
Considerations
Difficulty with vestibular processing or visual tracking makes it challenging to know where the body is in space, and can contribute to a child's fear of heights. Referral to an Occupational Therapist is indicated if there is concern about the child's sensory processing. Audiologists or Ear, Nose, and Throat (ENT) doctors may play a role if the child has vertigo or problems with the inner ear. Once medical causes have been ruled out or addressed, exposure can be used to treat this fear.

Exposures

○ Make a list of tall or high places you've been.

○ Listen to a story about going to a tall or high place.
Do an imaginal exposure of the child visiting a high place, such as a bridge or tall building, with the adult describing the scene in detail.

○ Watch a movie with scenes from high places.

H

○ Visit bridges.
Start with small bridges close to the ground and by viewing the bridge from afar before crossing it. Make the exposure more challenging by increasing the height and length of the bridge while decreasing proximity to a support person.

○ Visit a parking garage.
Walk or drive through the garage with the child, getting out to look over the railing at each level.

○ Ride an elevator up a tall building.
Have the child get off at each floor and look out a window.

○ Visit a two-story mall.
Have the child ride the escalator, use the elevator, or climb the stairs and look through railings to the floor below.

○ Stand on a balcony.
Begin by having the child stand close to a wall, moving closer to the outer edge of the balcony over subsequent exposures. Have the child look over the railing while holding it, then let go. Museums, town halls, sports arenas, and concert halls often have upper balconies available to the public.

○ Play on playground equipment.
Have the child use the swings, slide, monkey bars, or other elements that raise them off the ground. Start with the support person holding the child's hand if needed, then standing a step away, and then several steps away.

○ Go to an amusement park.
Have the child begin by watching others enjoy the rides, then ride the smaller rides, and eventually the taller ones, including the ferris wheel.

○ Go indoor rock climbing.
Have the child start low, moving further up the wall on subsequent visits.

○ Use virtual reality experiences and games.
Games and videos should be prescreened, and the amount of exposure to heights carefully administered by the therapist.

Also: Flying, Open Spaces

HOARDING
See: Getting Rid of Things

HORNETS
See: Bees

HOUSEHOLD PETS
See: Dogs, Frogs, Pet Escaping, Snakes

HURRICANES
See: Weather

HURTING ONESELF OR OTHERS
Considerations
Intrusive thoughts about self-harm and harming others are distinctly different from genuine suicidality and sociopathy. Intrusive thoughts are unwanted and frightening to the child, causing them to seek reassurance that they aren't going to act on them. The child might begin to avoid objects they imagine using or places they think the harm might take place. Truly suicidal thoughts, or pathological thoughts about harming others, tend to be less distressing to the person who is having them, and might even be viewed with relief or excitement. The therapist should conduct a thorough assessment of intrusive thoughts and their impact on the child. Intrusive thoughts can be treated with exposure, whereas desired thoughts are treated very differently.

Exposure for intrusive thoughts about harming oneself or others focuses on purposely spending time with feared objects in feared places. There is no attempt made to banish or undo uncomfortable thoughts, or to figure out whether the child "really" feels this way. Instead, the child learns to tolerate their discomfort, making clear that a thought is just a thought, with no power to hurt anyone. It is often necessary to meet with parents prior to beginning exposure for intrusive thoughts so they can learn to hold a neutral stance rather than inadvertently undoing exposures with reassurance.

H

Exposures

○ Write the scary thought.
The child might need to start by writing just part of the thought, or writing and immediately erasing it, prior to writing the intrusive thought, leaving it in place, and eventually hanging it somewhere.

○ Say the scary thought out loud.
Challenge the child to say the intrusive thought fast, slow, in a silly voice or with an accent. Have them move toward saying the entire thought with genuine feeling.

○ Write a story about the thought. Read the story out loud.

○ Be in a room with knives or other scary-seeming objects.
Have the child start at a comfortable distance before moving closer. Touch and then hold the objects.

○ Hold a knife to someone's wrist.
If, for example, the child fears killing themself or someone else with a knife, begin with an innocuous knife such as a butter knife, having the child hold it first to an adult's wrist and then to their own. Move to a sharper knife, first the back side, then the blade. The final level involves holding the knife while saying, "I'm going to cut you," "I'm going to stab you," or "I'm going to kill myself." This intervention may be alarming to the parent, so be sure to include them when doing the preparatory work of talking about the difference between thoughts, words, and actions.

○ Go to the place that scares you.
Have the child spend time in avoided places, such as the garage for the fear of hanging or a bathroom for the fear of an overdose. Gradually increase both distance from the support person and time spent in the feared place. Add feared objects such as a rope or pill bottle. Add the feared thought, "I could kill myself," having the child first think the thought on purpose, then say it out loud.

Also: Intrusive Thoughts, Uncertainty, Words and Phrases

H

1

ILLNESS
See: Health

IMPERFECTION
See: Losing, Mistakes, Perfectionism, Social Anxiety, Trying New Things

INJECTIONS
Considerations
You'd be hard pressed to find anyone who says they like injections, but for some children, the fear of getting an injection becomes overwhelming. Parents struggle with when and how to tell their child an injection is planned, and the debate about holding a child down to get it over with or not rages on. Children who fret days in advance of doctor's appointments and are then unable to cooperate with the procedure benefit from exposure, with the aim of being able to both talk about and go through the steps leading up to getting an injection without immediate and extreme panic.

Exposures

○ Play with a toy doctor kit.
  Take turns being the patient and the doctor. Include getting an injection.

○ Read a story that includes a child getting an injection.

○ Write a story about getting an injection.

○ Draw a picture of yourself getting an injection.

○ Imagine getting an injection.
  An adult can narrate the whole experience in detail.

○ Watch videos of people getting an injection.
There may be some value in watching people younger, older, or the same age as the child. Videos of acupuncture may also be useful.

○ Act out getting an injection.
This can be done using an open paper clip or a straight pin. Go through the motions of greeting the child, rubbing the injection-site with alcohol, pinching a bit of skin, and touching lightly with the "needle." Take turns giving and receiving pretend injections, allowing the child to choose which they want to do first.

○ Learn ways to manage fear and pain.
Practice pain and fear management techniques such as breathing, playing **I Spy** as a distraction, or rubbing the site with an ice cube prior to giving a fake injection. Try each technique a few times so the child can decide which they want to do on the day of the actual injection.

○ See someone else get an injection.
If possible, have a parent take the child with them when they get an injection or blood drawn. Have the child watch as much as they are able, although even if the child doesn't watch, just being there is an exposure.

Also: Blood, Dentists, Doctors

INSECTS
See: Bees, Bugs

INTERRUPTION
Considerations
Some children feel compelled to complete an action, and melt down when they are interrupted. This pattern is commonly seen in OCD and ASD. The aim of exposure for trouble with interruptions is to help the child learn to ride out their distress, and to see that nothing catastrophic happens. Exposure also helps children develop flexibility. As with all exposures, make every attempt to involve the child in choosing the challenges, and explain why they are being done.

Exposures

○ Play **Musical Chairs** or **Red Light, Green Light**.
Use games to help the child practice starting and stopping.

○ Pause during games.
Start with very short interruptions, even a few seconds, depending on the child's baseline. Use a distraction if needed, like doing a dance or singing a little song during the pause. Over time, move toward longer breaks and less compelling distractions. Breaks at set times will be easier than breaks that occur randomly, so move from one to the other.

○ Skip a page when reading, or stop before the end of a chapter.

○ Play **Ziiip!**
Take turns as the "Zipper" who has the power to make others briefly but immediately stop talking by looking at them and making a zipping motion across the lips. Each person's turn as Zipper can last 5–10 minutes, letting the child be the Zipper first. Ham up frustration at needing to stop speaking so abruptly.

○ Stop in the midst of daily activities.
Coach parents to pull over while driving, or pause in the middle of a meal, prompting the child to do a brief activity before resuming.

○ Play **Fast Again, Slow Again**.
Choose an imaginary play activity like school or store. Take turns shouting out, "Fast Again!" or "Slow Again!" to both interrupt and change the speed of play.

○ Turn off the television in the middle of a show.
Have the child start with a several-second interruption, increasing the length over time. If the pause will be longer than 20 seconds, have the child do a brief activity before returning to the show.

Also: Change in Plans, Unfairness

INTRUDERS
See: Baddies, Navigating Home Alone, Separation Anxiety

1

INTRUSIVE THOUGHTS
Considerations
Intrusive thoughts are highly distressing to children and parents, both of whom typically want nothing more than for them to stop. Exposure therefore seems counterintuitive, as we are asking the child to think their unwanted thoughts on purpose. Children often try to undo intrusive thoughts by avoiding, checking, and seeking reassurance. These safety behaviors must be closely monitored as they will undermine the efficacy of exposure.

Children can have intrusive thoughts about purposely harming themselves or others, inadvertent harm coming to someone they love, cheating, lying, stealing, unwanted sexual thoughts, illness and disease, suicide, divorce, accidents, and the impulse to do something mean, shameful, immoral, or destructive. Most children present to therapy with great embarrassment and shame about their thoughts, and it isn't unusual for children to be extremely hesitant to disclose them. It can be helpful to explain as part of psychoeducation that intrusive thoughts tend to be about things the child *doesn't* want, and they do not mean the child is a bad person.

Common Intrusive Thoughts

"Maybe I told a lie."

"I might have looked at someone's paper during the test."

"Maybe I stole something by mistake."

"I had a mean thought about someone."

"I'm not sure I believe in God."

"Maybe I'm gay."

"I might want to kill myself."

"I might be bad when I get older."

"I might have scratched or harmed something."

"I'm a bad person."

"I don't care about other people."

"I might have looked at someone's private parts."

"Someone I love is going to die."

"I'm going to die."

"My parents are going to get a divorce."

"I'm going to stop breathing in the night."

"My teacher (or someone else I know) is fat, or ugly, or stupid."

"That person wants to molest me."

"I'm dirty."

"I'm going to be late."

"I can't do this."

"I might throw up."

"I have to have that."

"Nobody likes me."

"I'm going to get sick and die."

"I can't be left alone."

"I'm going to develop an addiction."

"I can't eat anything that might make me sick."

Keep in mind that during exposure, you are targeting both the thoughts and the safety behaviors that have developed around them. Watch for undoing statements such as "…but I didn't" or "I won't," as well as elaborate attempts to figure out whether the child really means what they are thinking. An important part of exposure for intrusive thoughts has to do with developing tolerance for uncertainty, and learning to recognize that a thought is just a thought, with no predictive power. The same holds true for parents, who often need guidance on maintaining a supportive, neutral stance in the face of such disturbing thoughts.

Exposures

○ Write the scary thought.
The child may need to start with a single word and work toward writing the intrusive thought in its entirety. They may also need to write and then quickly erase the thought. In this case, the child can write on a whiteboard, in sand, or on a piece of paper they then crumple and throw away. Eventually, have the child write the thought in a more lasting way, and hang it up.

○ Say the scary thought out loud.
Challenge the child to add words until they are saying the whole thought. Have them play with volume by whispering the thought, saying it in a regular voice, and shouting it. Say it ten times fast. Use different voices, such as saying it like a baby, a dog, or the child's favorite character. Sing the thought to a familiar tune.

○ Make a recording of the scary thought and listen to it on a loop.
Have the child work up to saying the thought repeatedly with meaning and then listening for 10–15 minutes at a time.

○ Say the intrusive thought is possible.
Have the child add some version of, "It's always possible that…," or "I might…" to the start of an intrusive thought. Record, and have the child listen to the new sentence on a loop. For example, "It's always possible that I looked at my friend's paper" heard over and over again. It is also useful to have the child say, "Maybe I will, maybe I won't" following an intrusive thought. For example, "What if I stop breathing tonight? Maybe I will, maybe I won't," or "I might have looked at my friend's bottom at school today. Maybe I did, maybe I didn't."

○ Make up a poem or song about the scary thought.
Help the child to create a poem, limerick, or song that includes the intrusive thought. Try an app that turns recordings into raps.

O Use a **Token System**.

Have the family implement a Token System to move away from reassurance about intrusive thoughts. Here's how the system works: Start with three tokens a day. When a reassurance-seeking question is asked, the parent is to say, "That would be a token." The child then has a choice: they can give up a token to have the parent provide brief, qualified reassurance such as, "No one knows the future," or the child can say, "Never mind," foregoing a parental response to be able to keep the token. Unused tokens turn into points that can be cashed in for rewards. If the child uses all three tokens, then asks a fourth reassurance-seeking question, the parent can say, "I'm sorry, you're out of tokens," and not provide reassurance of any kind. The use of physical tokens is important as it interrupts the automaticity of asking and answering reassurance-seeking questions. Decrease the number of tokens available to the child over time. If the child is routinely using all available tokens, coach parents to give more neutral answers, even when the child has given up a token.

Also: Hurting Oneself or Others, Uncertainty, Words and Phrases

J

JABS
See: Injections

JUST RIGHT FEELING
Considerations
Needing to do something until it feels "just right" is a common presentation of OCD. For example, a child may feel the need to step into a room with their left foot first, or put on their socks in a very particular way. They might beseech their parents to say good-night again and again, or stand up and sit down multiple times before settling down to a meal. Sadly, trying to get something to feel "just right" can take a significant amount of time, causing frustration for both the child and the family. Exposure focuses on presenting triggering situations while inhibiting the urge to make them feel "right."

Exposures

○ Make a list of activities anxiety says need to be done "just right."
The child's list might include always stepping into a room with the left foot first, brushing their teeth in a certain way, or arranging objects in a particular order on the dresser. Organize the list from the least to the most compelling. Starting with the least compelling, do each activity the "wrong" way.

○ Delay making something "just right."
Start with a several-second delay, extending the time until the child is able to fully walk away even though they feel "not right."

○ Use a timer to limit re-doing.
For example, setting a timer during homework limits re-writing and erasing, and teaches the child to move on even though they don't yet feel "right."

○ Put your things in the "wrong" place or un-organize something.

○ Touch something a different number of times than the urge says, stopping before it feels "right."

○ When something feels "just right" do it once more to make it "wrong" on purpose.

○ Use **3–2–1–Stop**.
When caught in a re-doing loop, have the child count down to stop the behavior, even if it doesn't feel "right."

○ Play **Dice It Wrong**.
Roll two dice at the start of the day. The number rolled indicates how many "just wrongs" to accumulate that day, with an incentive for meeting the goal. This exposure works best if the child logs the things done "wrong," both to keep track of them and to increase their awareness of consciously stopping when something feels wrong.

Also: Asymmetry, Numbers, Perfectionism, Uncertainty

J

KIDNAPPERS
See: Baddies, Crowds, Navigating Home Alone, Separation Anxiety

KILLING
See: Hurting Oneself or Others, Intrusive Thoughts

KNIVES
See: Hurting Oneself or Others, Intrusive Thoughts

L

LATENESS
Considerations
Children can become hyper-focused on lateness for a variety of reasons. For some, sensory processing differences make it more comfortable to be in a room first, allowing noise and visual clutter to increase slowly around them, rather than entering an already-busy space. Other children become fixated on punctuality as part of a pattern of perfectionism, or because they fear embarrassment or reprimand if they arrive late. Understanding what is causing the fear will help you craft an individualized exposure plan.

Exposures

○ Practice feeling unsure about time.
Instruct the parent to answer the first reassurance-seeking question in a qualified way with something along the lines of, "I have no reason to think we'll be late, but I can't control traffic," or "Maybe we'll be on time and maybe not. It's hard to know for sure." The second time, the parent can say, "I already answered that." And the third time, "That's a worry question. I'm going to help you by not answering it."

○ Put away the clocks.
Have the parent cover or remove clocks and turn over devices. Systematically decrease the number of times the parent will tell the child what time it is.

○ Imagine being late.
Describe to the child what would actually happen if they were late, including walking in, people looking at the child, or being spoken to.

○ Leave home at the right time, not the time anxiety says.
Coach the parent to leave home at the appropriate time rather than allowing anxiety to dictate what time the family will leave.

- Get rid of extra time.
  Reduce and eventually eliminate time cushions, including waking up earlier than necessary.

- Arrive late on purpose.
  Start with a low-stakes situation like a visit with a family member. Move to higher-stakes situations like being late to sports practice or school. Make sure the child knows they are late.

- Be later than you intended by counting to 100 before going in.
  When arriving on time at their destination, have the child wait at the door and count to 100 before going in so they are entering a little later than intended. Slow down the counting over time.

Also: Mistakes, Perfectionism, Social Anxiety, Uncertainty

LIGHTNING
See: Weather

LOSING

Considerations

Having trouble losing is common, particularly among 4–7-year-olds. This is often due to the faulty belief that losing means the child is deficient in some way. Difficulty losing can, however, continue beyond this developmental period, or be so disruptive that the child cannot successfully participate in family life or activities with friends.

Exposure to losing works to develop three things: frustration tolerance; an understanding that practice leads to greater skill, also known as a growth mindset; and positive socialization skills for both winning and losing. To supplement exposure therapy, the therapist might teach the difference between games of skill, like checkers, and games of luck, like War. Because children who have trouble losing often overreact to winning, too, direct teaching about courteous conduct and reading books about winning and losing can also support exposure.

Exposures

- Play cooperative games where no one wins or loses.

L

○ Make games less frustrating by agreeing to change the rules.
Work together with the child to alter the rules of a game to make it less frustrating. For example, in the game **Candyland**, you might remove the pink cards that send players backward. Over time, re-introduce the cards and rules you modified. **Snakes and Ladders** is brutal for sending players backward; play at your own risk.

○ Play the card game **War**.
This game exposes children to the possibility of losing with every round. Model appropriate responses such as, "Oh well," or "My luck is running out," or good-natured silence. Break the game into a predetermined number of rounds versus playing until someone is out of cards. Early on, you might say, "That was fun!" and end the game without counting to see who has the most cards. Later, you can include a card count, which makes clear that someone has won and someone has lost.

○ Learn about cheating.
When treating a child who cheats, the therapist can start by playing without commenting on the cheating. Begin exposure to the possibility of losing by commenting on the cheating in a neutral way, later adding that it is less fun to play when cheating happens. Ultimately, the therapist and child can decide together, "Are we going to play with cheating today or without?"

○ Talk about the game coming to an end.
Play a game, pausing before reaching the conclusion. As you approach the end of a game the child is losing, say, "It looks like we are close to the end of the game, and I'm in front. What do you think we should do?" You might add, "Do you feel up to seeing who's going to win or should we stop?" Teach parents to do this as well. When you are working with a child who has an aversion to losing, this technique exposes the child to the possibility of losing and gives them a verbal, adaptive alternative to a meltdown.

○ Play games for longer stretches.
For example, you might play **Go Fish** for three turns each and then stop, regardless of how the game is going. Then play for five turns each, and stop. Then seven turns each, adding turns until you are playing a full game.

○ Practice losing on purpose.
Decide ahead of time who is going to win and who is going to lose, either by coin toss or by taking turns. If it's the child's turn to lose, talk about how they can make that happen and what they will say and do at the end of the game.

L

○ Practice respectful winning and losing.
Teach respectful conduct, for example saying, "Good job," or "Nice move" when losing, and remaining kind when winning. Consider rewarding the child for using these skills. For example, the child might take an extra turn, get an extra point, or be the one to choose the next game if they remain courteous regardless of what is happening in the game.

Also: Change in Plans, Mistakes, Perfectionism, Trying New Things, Unfairness

LYING (INADVERTENT)
Considerations
Children who are afraid of inadvertently lying typically qualify what they are saying with expressions of doubt such as, "I think," "maybe," or "I don't know." Using qualifiers is often firmly entrenched by the time the child presents for therapy, as it is easy for parents to initially ignore these verbal quirks. Concern about inadvertent lying is typically an intrusive thought, occurring in the context of OCD. It will not be surprising to learn that exposure involves playing with uncertainty and lying on purpose. There is no evidence that this type of exposure leads to problematic lying, a finding important to share with parents who, understandably, might find intentional lying concerning.

Exposures

○ Practice **No-Waffling** times.
Designate brief stretches of time during which the child is to speak without qualifiers. If they use a qualifier, the adult can say, "Re-do," or "Try again" and the child needs to repeat what they said without the qualifier. Extend the length of No-Waffling time.

○ Play **Wacky Trivia**.
Whoever answers the most questions *wrong* wins.

○ Play **Two Truths and a Lie**.
Each player makes three statements, only two of which are true. The other players have to guess which is the lie. Coach the child to make their lies plausible so it's hard for the other players to guess.

L

Rapid-Fire Q&A

"What's your favorite kind of ice cream?"

"How many siblings do you have?"

"What did you dress up as for Halloween last year?"

"What did you eat for breakfast today?"

"What's your favorite movie?"

"What book did you read most recently?"

"How many pets have you ever had?"

"What's the name of a dog that lives on your street?"

"What's your favorite color?"

"What color underwear are you wearing?"

"Did you like your dinner last night?"

"What do you want for your next birthday?"

"How old are you?"

"Have you ever told a lie?"

"What show do you think is funny?"

"What's a show you liked when you were younger but not anymore?"

"What's your favorite smell?"

"What's the worst smell ever?"

"Where would you like to go on vacation?"

"Who's your favorite superhero?"

"What grade are you in?"

"What do you like best about school?"

"What's the worst part about school?"

"How many grandparents do you have?"

"What's your favorite animal?"

"What's an animal you think is annoying?"

"Where's the best place to sit in a car?"

"Where's the best place to sit when you are watching a show?"

"Which musical instruments can you play?"

"What three sports do you like?"

"What time do you go to bed?"

"What's your favorite thing to drink?"

"What time do you leave for school?"

"Which friend would you like to spend time with?"

"What's something that belongs to someone else that you wish was yours?"

"If you could get a pet, what kind would you want?"

"What is something you have made by yourself?"

"What's your favorite thing to do at recess?"

"What season do you like best?"

"What year is it?'

"Do you like my shirt?"

"If you had to choose just one, would you rather have a dog or a cat?"

"Who is your best friend?"

"How many toes do you have?"

"What is something that's gross?"

"What animal would make a terrible pet?"

"What is something with a zipper?"

○ Play **Rapid-Fire Q&A**.

In this game, the adult asks a string of questions for the child to answer quickly and without qualification. Be sure to include questions that have a definite, true answer as well as those that do not. Due to the difficulty of answering quickly, some of the child's answers are likely to be untrue, especially if you include a no-take-backs rule. Ask a mix of fact and opinion

L

questions, knowing that questions about favorites are especially challenging for children afraid of inadvertent lying. Take turns reading and answering questions, allowing the therapist or parent to model giving arbitrary answers, taking guesses, and settling for partial answers, all without qualifiers. Do five to ten questions, one right after another, before switching places.

○ Tell a white lie.
Plan ahead of time for the child to tell a white lie. For example, the child can misreport who they played with at recess, or compliment someone on an item of clothing they don't really like.

Also: Intrusive Thoughts, Perfectionism, Uncertainty

L

M

MAKING DECISIONS
Considerations
Children who have trouble with decision-making often fear making the "wrong" choice, going down a rabbit hole of anticipatory regret. They seek certainty for simple choices, wanting a guarantee that things will turn out well. Adults often accommodate by removing choices or choosing for the child. Another common mistake is to allow the child to endlessly waffle, or to pepper them with questions like, "Well, which do you want?" Encouraging a child who gets stymied by simple choices to make a list of pros and cons is also counterproductive as it reinforces the notion that there is a "right" choice. Strategies like these might help the child feel better in the moment, but make the problem worse in the long run.

Of course, periodic indecisiveness is perfectly normal, requiring nothing more than empathy. It is only when trouble making decisions begins to interfere with daily functioning that we turn to exposure. Keep in mind that we are working on the global problem of anxious indecision, not a particular instance of it. Teaching the child to say to themself something along the lines of, "It's okay to not know" and, "Any decision is better than no decision" can help with the thinking mistakes fueling this particular fear.

Exposures

○ Read a book about children making decisions.

○ Play strategy games.
Games like checkers or chess require repeated decision-making, as do story-telling games.

○ Use chance to make decisions.
When there are just two choices, have the child flip a coin. When there are more than two choices, use a die or a spinner, or have the child write the options on folded slips of paper then pick one at random.

○ Practice making decisions.
Begin with humorous choices such as, "Would you like oatmeal or dirt for breakfast?" Gradually increase the difficulty of questions. For example, move from, "Would you like eggs or pickle soup?" to "Would you like your toast cut in two pieces or four?" and finally, "Would you like [a food the child likes] or [another food the child likes]?"

○ Use a time limit for decision-making.
If the child has not made a choice within the designated time, shift to having them use chance, like a coin toss, to decide. Do not decide for the child.

○ Make your own decisions for just a little while.
Start with a small window of decision-making. For example, over the next hour the child is responsible for their own decisions while the rest of the day is up to the parent. Or, the child decides their breakfast only. Expand the decision-making window over time.

○ Practice making quick decisions.
Teach the child to make a quick decision for unimportant things like what to eat for breakfast. Over time they will see that even if they don't love what they chose, they can handle it. For many things, there is no "right" decision.

Also: Perfectionism, Uncertainty

MASCOTS
See: Costumed Characters

MASKS
See: Baddies, Costumed Characters

MEDIA
Considerations
Children sometimes develop oversized fears related to books, movies, or computers because they think they might inadvertently see something "inappropriate" or scary. Sometimes this fear develops after encountering something scary or disconcerting, and sometimes it occurs without a triggering event.

As with many fears, the goal is to teach the child to follow basic safety guidelines rather than the strict limits imposed by their anxiety. If the child is afraid

M

of a book or movie the parent sees as inappropriate, tailor the exposure to just the scene or character that has gotten stuck for the child rather than having them read or watch the whole thing.

Computers are a little different from other types of media because there are real dangers for children online. Exposure related to internet use must be paired with an age-appropriate plan for online safety. The stipulation that the internet is accessed only in shared spaces is a commonsense rule for children, as is the understanding that parents will have access to all usernames and passwords.

Exposures

BOOKS

O Say the name of the book.

O Look at the book.
Move from keeping the book on a shelf to having it out where it will be seen more often. Have the child hold the book without opening it. Read just the front and back covers.

O Open the book to a random page.
Have the child open the book at random, then linger on the page, scanning it without fully reading. Challenge the child to find all the *t*'s, for example, or to count the number of times the word *and* appears. Progress to reading individual paragraphs at random, and then full pages.

O Look at the art in the book.

O Read a scary section of the book.
The passage will need to be prescreened by an adult. Have the child read the same passage several times. If necessary, start by having the child read every other word, or read the passage backward or in a funny voice, before moving to fully reading it.

O Read the whole book.

INTERNET

O Watch someone open a scary-but-safe website.
Work toward having the child open the website themself.

O Look around on a scary-but-safe website.
Start with a support person in the room, gradually moving them away until they are out of the room.

M

○ Say the name of the movie.

○ Look at a poster for the movie.

○ Watch a trailer for the movie.
Have the child watch a trailer for the movie, then challenge them to make their own trailer.

○ Watch parts of the movie.
Show the child sections of the movie, jumping around, fast forwarding, and playing sections backward. Start with viewing just a couple of minutes at a time. View without sound if a smaller step is needed.

○ Watch a scene with a scary character.
Cue up the scene and freeze the image for the child to look at it. Move from poking fun at the character to talking about the character or scene in more serious ways. Watch small parts of the scary scene before watching the whole scene.

○ Watch the whole movie.

Also: Baddies, Dolls, Navigating Home Alone, Separation Anxiety, Uncertainty, Words and Phrases

MEDICAL PROCEDURES
Considerations
Medical procedures, although sometimes necessary, can be traumatizing. We do not intentionally expose children to things that are painful, legitimately frightening, or too difficult for them to understand. Therefore, treatment for children who have to undergo medical procedures should first be supportive and trauma informed. However, we can use exposure for visiting medical professionals and tolerating being around the objects they use. The purpose is to reduce the child's fear while supporting them to function despite the difficult experience.

See: Blood, Dentists, Doctors, Injections

MEDICINE (FEAR OF CONTAMINATION)
See: Contamination

M

MEDICINE (FEAR OF DEFECT, ILLNESS, FAILURE)
See: Health, Mistakes, Perfectionism

MEDICINE (FEAR OF HARM)
See: Drugs

MEDICINE (FEAR OF SWALLOWING)
Considerations
Before initiating exposure for the fear of swallowing pills, make sure there is no substantive reason for the fear such as oral motor planning challenges or the inability to fully sense one's mouth. Children with these issues should work with a Speech and Language Pathologist or an Occupational Therapist first. Additionally, children with thyroid dysfunction often feel like there is a lump in their throat, which should be evaluated by a medical provider. When there is no medical basis for the fear of pill-swallowing, the following exposures, presented steadily and patiently, almost always do the trick.

Exposures

O Watch videos of children swallowing pills.

O Write or draw directions for how to swallow a pill.

O Compare the size of a bite of food to the size of a pill.
  Have the child take a normal bite of a regularly eaten food, chew it, and then spit it out. Compare the chewed-up bite of food with the size of the pill the child needs to swallow.

O Swallow pill-sized candies.
  Use small, smooth candies like Tic Tacs or cupcake sprinkles. Start with whatever size the child is able to swallow whole, even if it means cutting the candy in half or soaking it to reduce its size. Have the child swallow that size several times, then make it a little bigger. Continue increasing the size until the child is able to swallow a pill-sized candy. This can be done with or without water. If water is being used, make sure the child is not melting the candy in their mouth before swallowing it.

Also: Choking

MISTAKES
Considerations
Difficulty tolerating mistakes often appears in children who have a significant challenge in some other area, such as speech or motor skills. Children with developmental differences often become reactive to challenges because their coping skills are repeatedly tested and eventually used up.

There are also children without developmental challenges who are highly sensitive to mistakes, leading to tears, meltdowns, and missing out on new activities. Children who cannot tolerate mistakes often swing between overconfidence and underconfidence, gleefully announcing when they get something right and feeling utterly abject at the first sign of struggle. Angry outbursts are common, as is blaming other people and insisting that the activity they are having trouble with is "stupid" or "boring."

While children can be hard on themselves without unrealistic parental expectations, parents do play a key role in normalizing mistakes. Often parents inadvertently reinforce the child's notion that they are either good at something or bad at it, and err on the side of overpraising which, paradoxically, undermines the child's inclination to take chances. Parents can be encouraged to model acceptance of their own mistakes, and to develop a family culture that includes taking on challenges, accepting imperfection, and doing hard things on purpose. There is a wide selection of books on developing a growth mindset that nicely supports exposure work.

Exposures

○ Talk about people's mistakes in movies and books.
The adult can maintain a neutral stance by saying something like, "Oh, wow. It looks like they made a mistake. I wonder what's going to happen next."

○ Write a story about making mistakes.
In early versions, the story can be about someone else. Eventually have the child put themselves in the story, then read the story aloud several times.

○ Count other people's mistakes.
Have the child subtly tally classmates' mistakes during a set period of time to normalize making mistakes. This can also be done on family outings, at sporting events, and while traveling in the car. Make sure the child understands that mistake-counting happens only for brief periods of time, and only as part of exposure, so as not to reinforce policing or judging others. Model an air of sympathy, neutrality, and kindness around mistakes, "Oops. I bet they didn't mean to do that."

M

○ Color outside the lines on purpose.
Have the child make and then leave intentional mistakes without correcting them or throwing the project away. Do this first at home in the context of play, then on a homework paper, and finally at school. After the child has learned to tolerate intentional mistakes, encourage them to also leave unintentional mistakes in place.

○ Misspell a word during a game.
After misspelling a word during a game, have the child misspell on something with higher stakes, like homework.

○ Make a math mistake on purpose.

○ Answer a question wrong in class on purpose.

○ Leave mistakes on schoolwork.
Begin by limiting erasures, such as with a Token System, or roll a die to determine the number of fixes. For children trying to form letters perfectly or write exactly on the line, talk about the goal of legibility rather than perfection.

○ Leave a mistake on a page, with a single cross-out and the correction written above or below the line.

○ Use a pen instead of a pencil.

○ Skip problems you don't know and continue on.

○ Make a mistake on purpose while playing a sport.
For example, the child might decide to miss a basket or miss a catch.

Also: Apologies, Just Right Feeling, Losing, Perfectionism, Social Anxiety

MONSTERS
See: Baddies

MOTION SICKNESS
Considerations
Motion sickness is an unfortunate reality for some children. There are tricks to reduce it, such as looking forward rather than to the side, watching the horizon, refraining from reading in the car, eating ginger, sucking mints, staying

M

hydrated, wearing motion-sickness bands, and distracting yourself with music, conversation, or car games. When the fear of motion-sickness rises to the level of extreme distress or even refusal to travel by car, exposure is needed. Please keep in mind that what you are exposing the child to is car travel, not feeling ill. Steps should still be taken to keep the child as comfortable as possible.

Exposures

- Spend time in a parked car.
  Have the child play a game, read a book, sing a song, or talk to a parent, all without electronic devices.

- Ride in a car for a very short distance.
  Make the drive as short as necessary, which may mean starting with up and down the driveway or to the end of the block and back, increasing distance over time.

- Ride in a car with more people.
  Add people to the car, moving from the child and one parent to the inclusion of siblings or friends.

- Go someplace fun.
  Move from short jaunts to high-interest destinations to longer trips and places of less interest to the child.

Also: Uncertainty, Vomiting

MOVIES
See: Baddies, Media

M

N

NATURAL DISASTERS
See: Weather

NAVIGATING HOME ALONE

Considerations

A surprising number of children have fears that prevent them from moving freely around their own home. Parents, siblings, and pets all get recruited to go upstairs, downstairs, or into the bathroom with the child. On the bright side, this is a relatively easy fear to treat as all of the challenges can be done at home over the course of a normal day. Families who practice daily often report quick success, giving them the boost they need to take on other, more complicated fears.

Exposures

○ Play near a parent.
  Increase the distance between parent and child. This may mean having the child play in a doorway before moving to another room, out of sight of the parent. Or the child may go up half a flight of stairs in front of the parent before being able to go up alone.

○ Do a **Challenge Race**.
  Give the child a challenge to do in a separate space before returning. For example: touch every doorknob, twirl around in every room, draw a favorite character, or read a chapter.

○ Use sound rather than sight to know where your parent is.
  Use sound between the parent and child while the child goes to a separate part of the home. The parent and child can do a call and response, or sing a song together so the child knows where the parent is. Gradually fade the sound connection by having the adult remain silent, with notice, for increasingly long stretches of time.

○ Carry a string.
  Have the child go to a separate space carrying a string that is held on the other end by the parent. Increase the challenge by having the child put down the string for a period of time.

○ Play **Find It**.
  Take turns hiding and finding a small object, doing both the hiding and finding alone. Intensify the challenge by expanding the range and complexity of hiding places, increasing the amount of time needed to find the object.

○ Play **Hide and Seek**.
  Increase the challenge by extending the search area and by hiding in harder-to-find spots.

○ Do a **Scavenger Hunt**.
  Have the parent hide clues around the home, or challenge the child to find objects such as something that smells good, something that reminds you of summer, something colorful, or something you made. Make sure the challenges require going to the far reaches of the home alone.

○ Do daily **Alone Time**.
  Have the child spend time alone in a room for a set period of time without calling for the parent or coming out of the room. The child can draw, write, or play. Avoid the use of books or electronics as they can be too absorbing, reducing the effectiveness of the exposure. Start with the child's baseline tolerance of being alone in a room, even if only for a few seconds, and increase gradually but persistently over time until the child is able to stay alone in a room for 20 minutes. Work with the distance between the child and parent, eventually having the parent remain on a different floor or step outside briefly.

Also: Baddies, Separation Anxiety

NEEDLES
See: Injections

NEW EXPERIENCES
See: Trying New Things

N

NIGHT
See: Dark

NO
Considerations
Some children have great difficulty accepting "No" for an answer. Others give a knee-jerk, "No" to suggestions or requests. Each of these scenarios is addressed elsewhere.

See: Change in Plans, Mistakes, Social Anxiety, Speaking, Trying New Things, Uncertainty, Unfairness

NOISES
Considerations
Fear of noises often occurs in children who have sensory processing differences or exceptionally sensitive hearing. Children may avoid places where they have experienced auditory discomfort in the past, and places where they anticipate discomfort. If the child has not already been assessed, referral to an Occupational Therapist or audiologist is recommended.

Just like we don't treat a fear of injections by repeatedly giving injections, we don't treat the fear of loud noises with intentional exposure to uncomfortably loud sounds. The focus of exposure is, instead, on the fear. This means we have the child practice putting themself into situations where there could be loud sounds, helping them acclimate to the possibility of noise. Keep in mind that noises made by others are likely to be more challenging than noises made by the child. As exposure progresses, encourage parents to withdraw reassurance about noise.

Exposures to feared sounds are done initially with ear protection or noise generators as needed, at the child's discretion. Be aware that while ear protection does help with challenging noises, it can ultimately make smaller noises stand out. Noise-generating earphones use white noise or relaxing music to mask the sounds of the environment. Both can be helpful at the start of treatment, and both can be faded as the child's sensory system matures.

N

Exposures

O Make a list of noisy places or noises you can't control.
   The list might include: school cafeteria, all-school assemblies, fire alarms, gym class, public bathrooms, trucks driving by, the schoolbus, sporting events, home appliances, or movies. Have the child arrange these from least to most scary, and work together to craft an exposure plan from the least scary on up.

O Write a story about a child who learned to manage loud noises.

O Visit a noisy place with ear protection.
   Have the child start at a comfortable distance, then gradually move closer to the source of the noise. Increase the length of time spent in the location. For children with only mild sensory challenges, encourage the eventual removal of ear protection.

O Attend a noisy gathering.
   This might be a school assembly or birthday party. Start by having the child stay outside the event space with a support person before standing in an open doorway and then entering the room.

O Play **Noise Bingo**.
   Create a Bingo card with places or situations the child is currently avoiding such as: go into a public bathroom, turn on a hand dryer, flush a toilet, participate in gym class, ride the schoolbus, walk past a truck with its engine running, or eat lunch in the cafeteria. Reward the child for checking off rows, and eventually the whole card.

O Make music with someone.
   Experiment with different musical instruments or household objects that make noise.

Also: Uncertainty

NUMBERS
Considerations
Children can get fixated on numbers in several ways. They may feel as though they need to perform actions a certain number of times. They might get triggered by a particular number and have to perform an undoing ritual when it is encountered. Or they might count as they do things, needing to track where they are numerically at all times. There is, of course, nothing wrong with having

N

a favorite or least-favorite number. Exposure is only used when the child's dedication to a number, or avoidance of a number, interferes with day-to-day life.

Exposures
FOR NUMBER FIXATION

O Roll a die to decide.
Use a die to determine how many times something will be done rather than doing it the number of times the child is fixated on.

O Do plus one or minus one.
Add to or subtract from the number the child is fixated on, and have them do things that many times.

O Sing a song or count by twos while doing something.
Help the child craft an intentional distraction to make it harder to keep track of how many times something is being done.

O Stop when you hear the sound.
For children who count during activities to ensure that they are doing them the "right" number of times, interrupt at random with a bell or keyword. The challenge is to stop when the bell sounds or the word is spoken, regardless of what number the child is on.

FOR TRIGGERING NUMBERS

O Make number art.
Support the child to create art focused on the triggering number. Draw it in bubble letters and color it in. Write the number in glue and cover it with glitter. Sculpt the number out of clay. Leave the art on display.

O Do a **Hidden Picture** activity with the difficult number.

O Listen to or make up a song featuring the difficult number.

O Wear a shirt with the number on it.

O Play **Today's Number Is!**
To play Today's Number Is! draw a number from 1–20 out of a bag to determine how many exposures related to the triggering number the child will do that day. For example, if the child avoids 13, and they draw a 6 from the bag, they will do six challenges related to the number 13 such as 1) wear 13 hair

N

ties around their wrist, 2) eat 13 blueberries with their breakfast, 3) pack 13 pencils for school, 4) sit in the 13th row of the schoolbus, 5) say hello to 13 people, and 6) have 13 pretzels for their after-school snack.

Also: Asymmetry, Just Right Feeling, Words and Phrases

NURSES

See: Blood, Dentists, Doctors, Injections

N

OCEAN

See: Birds, Dangerous Animals, Noises, Water Immersion

OLDER PEOPLE

See: Differentness

OPEN SPACES

Considerations

Anxiety about open spaces can be triggered by large indoor spaces or expansive outdoor spaces as both have indefinite boundaries. Difficulty with vestibular processing or visual tracking is sometimes a confounding variable as these make it challenging to know where one's body is in space. If the child has sensory processing issues, consider referral to an Occupational Therapist. If the child has vertigo or other problems with the inner ear, audiologists or ENT doctors may also play a role, as may physical therapists. Once medical issues have been ruled out or addressed, exposure can help with the fear of open spaces.

Exposures

○ Imagine large open spaces.
Describe for the child in detail what the space looks like. You can talk about large fields, mountain ranges, or sports arenas, using either real or imagined spaces. Over subsequent imaginal exposures, insert the child into the open space.

○ Watch a video or movie showing open spaces.
The movie will need to be prescreened by an adult. Child-centric videos or animations will be less challenging than actual footage or documentary-style videos, so consider moving from one to the other.

○ Visit a building with high ceilings.
The visit can occur at a supermarket, indoor pool, town hall, or museum. Start by having the child stand in the doorway and look in. Over subsequent visits, walk inside, then increase the length of time spent in the open space.

○ Visit a large open space.
Take the child to a large open space such as a field or empty parking lot. Initially just drive by, then stop and observe the space from inside the car. On subsequent visits, open the car door and step out. Gradually move further into the open space, extending the amount of time spent there while also increasing the distance between the child and support person.

Also: Crowded Places, Panic, Separation Anxiety

OVERWIPING
See: Contamination, Wiping

O

PANIC
Considerations
The purpose of exposure for panic is to desensitize to the thoughts, sensations, places, and activities associated with prior episodes. The exposures listed below should be repeated in a variety of places, starting with locations the child sees as safe, such as home, and moving to more difficult locations. While we aren't trying to trigger a full-blown panic episode, one might occur during exposure, in which case, the therapist or parent can support the child to ride it out without leaving. The aim is to learn to tolerate uncomfortable physical sensations and stay put using self-calming techniques instead of immediately going home. Support parents to reduce reassurances that the child isn't going to have an episode.

Exposures

○ Read a fictional story about a child experiencing and overcoming panic.

○ Create a detailed story about experiencing panic and riding it out.
   In early versions, the story can be about someone else. Eventually have the child put themselves in the story and read it aloud several times.

○ Put on someone else's glasses and walk around.
   Have the child try to find a hidden object, play **Simon Says,** or do another activity likely to trigger disorientation as this is often associated with panic.

○ Spin in circles to make yourself dizzy.

○ Get your heart pounding.
   Have the child use a jump rope, run up and down the stairs, dance, or do jumping jacks to increase their heart rate, as this can feel disconcerting or scary to an anxious child.

○ Get hot on purpose.
   Have the child exercise with a coat on or sit in a small room with a space heater, as feeling overheated can be a trigger for panic.

○ Breathe heavily.
Have the child take quick inhalations and long, forceful exhalations to induce lightheadedness.

○ Breathe through a straw.
Have the child breathe through a straw while pinching their nose closed. Start with just one breath, gradually adding more over time. It may only take a few breaths to trigger the feeling that there is not enough air.

○ Watch a video of a moving spiral or something rolling and churning.

○ Listen to the sound of a racing heart.

○ Wear a snug scarf.
Wearing a scarf a little tighter than preferred will trigger a constricted feeling around the neck, another sensation associated with panic.

○ Eat something that makes you feel too full, then move around.

○ Go for a boat ride.

○ Read in the car.

○ Have a **Pretend Vomit Competition**.
Whoever is most convincing wins.

○ Go back to the places you've felt panicky before.
Have the child visit places they associate with panic. Increase the amount of time spent in each place, fading the support person.

○ Say a scary thought out loud.
This exposure invites in the intrusive thoughts associated with panic without trying to disprove or undo them. For example, have the child state out loud, "I'm not going to be able to escape," or "I might go crazy." Watch for reassurance-seeking or un-doing self-talk.

Anxiety in the Body
✓ Dizziness
✓ Visual disturbances
✓ Dry mouth
✓ Choking sensation
✓ Shortness of breath
✓ Heart pounding
✓ Upset stomach
✓ Sweaty armpits
✓ Sweaty hands
✓ Derealization
✓ Feeling the need to pee or poop
✓ Tingling in hands or feet

○ Leave good luck items at home.
This exposure is for children who carry objects they think will protect them, such as a cell phone or water bottle. Start by adding distance between the

P

child and the object, then limit the places the child is able to bring the object, eventually eliminating it entirely.

Also: Choking, Dizziness, Intrusive Thoughts, Navigating Home Alone, Separation Anxiety, Uncertainty, Vomiting

PEOPLE
See: Baddies, Differentness, Public Speaking, Social Anxiety, Speaking

PERFECTIONISM
Considerations
Perfectionism is the intolerance of performance that falls short of an unreasonably high standard. There are numerous factors that contribute to this rigid cognitive style, including family history, which means that treatment often needs to be multifaceted.

Perfectionistic children want to be held in high esteem. They may put off a task for fear of it coming out poorly. Conversely, they may work on something far longer than necessary, trying to achieve perfection. Interrupting this plan typically causes distress. Reassuring the child that their work is wonderful, which adults often do, inadvertently reinforces the child's need to always shine. Exposure works to familiarize the child with doing things imperfectly, helping them see that disappointment eventually dissipates, and nothing catastrophic happens. There is a catch-22 inherent in these exposures, as the only way to succeed is to err.

Exposures

○ Wear something that clashes.
Have the child wear mismatched socks on purpose or an outfit that doesn't go together.

○ Leave your hair messy.
Have the child leave their hair uncombed, or style it in an uneven way such as a crooked part or lopsided braids.

○ Wear a shirt with a stain on it.

○ Disorganize something.

P

○ Pronounce something wrong on purpose.
Move from having the child do this in the home to doing it at school or in other public places.

○ Do something you think you are "bad at."

○ Spend less time on homework.
Use a clock or timer to systematically decrease time spent on assignments. Have the child stop, even if the work doesn't feel done.

○ Make mistakes on purpose.
Have the child roll a single die to determine how many intentional errors they will make that day.

○ Write something wrong on purpose.
Have the child leave a writing error such as a misspelled word or imperfectly formed letter on an assignment without fixing or erasing it.

○ Talk about something you don't know anything about.
An adult can ask questions to which the child does not know the answers. Support the child to stay in the conversation even though they don't feel like an expert.

○ Turn in work that isn't finished.

○ Leave a school supply at home.
Have the child start with something relatively unimportant like a spare eraser, and move toward an important item, like a pencil.

○ Arrive somewhere late.

○ Learn something new.
Some children find learning harder when someone is teaching them. Others find it more difficult when working alone. Start with whichever scenario is easier for the child.

○ Do something you typically avoid.
Help the child identify activities they avoid because they seem too hard or are "boring," which is often code for unfamiliar or difficult. Have the child begin by doing the avoided activity alone, then in front of others.

○ Make an awkward mistake.
Have the child knock over a drink, a chair, or pile of papers, first alone, then in front of others. Consider having the child watch someone else make these mistakes first.

P

- **Collect No's.**
  Have the child make unreasonable requests, such as, "Can I have $100?," or "Can I ride my skateboard through the mall?" Begin with whichever is easier, familiar people or strangers. A support person should be on hand to help identify a friendly stranger.

Also: Just Right Feeling, Losing, Mistakes, Social Anxiety

PET ESCAPING
Considerations
Children who live in fear of a pet escaping need eyes on their pet at all times, continually monitoring the animal's whereabouts and the state of various entryways. Exposure focuses on the safety behaviors the child is using to keep tabs on their pet and keep their own uncertainty at bay.

Exposures

- Read a fictional story about a pet escaping.

- Write a story about a pet escaping.
  Start with a story about any pet, working toward a story about the child's pet. The story can be made up, or it can describe something that actually happened.

- Use all the doors.
  This exposure can be used for children who prevent family members from using certain entryways for fear that their pet will escape. Systematically add entryways until all are in use, watching for safety behaviors such as reassurance-seeking or checking.

- Stand back when people are coming and going.
  Make pet management the parent's responsibility when people are entering or exiting the home. Start with having the child observe the parent opening or closing the door, then move the child out of sight of the door, and then further away, all while not holding or being reassured about the pet.

- Check on doors, locks, latches, and your pet's safety less often.
  Challenge the child to systematically decrease checking of all kinds until they are no longer checking. Increase difficulty by having someone open or close doors, or take the animal out of the home, without subsequent reassurance or checking.

- Let a parent be responsible for the comings and goings of an outdoor pet.

P

PETS
See: Birds, Dogs, Frogs, Pet Escaping, Snakes

PICKY EATING
See: Selective Eating

PILLS
See: Drugs, Medicine

POOP/POOPING
See: Contamination, Toileting, Wiping

POTTY SEAT
See: Toileting, Wiping

PUBERTY
See: Growing Up

PUBLIC SPEAKING
Considerations
Fear of public speaking is nearly ubiquitous, and typically doesn't get targeted for treatment unless it is coupled with panic or school refusal. As with virtually all forms of exposure, frequent practice is key. Aim to have the child practice speaking in public as close to every day as possible, not just the handful of times the teacher might assign an oral project. The initial goal is not to get rid of the fear but to have the child learn to speak even though they feel nervous.

Exposures

○ Practice public speaking at home.
  Have the child give presentations to family members, extended family, friends, and neighbors.

P

○ Participate in a presentation without speaking.
Have the child participate in a presentation nonverbally by pointing to a poster or using their hands to demonstrate how something works.

○ Answer a question in front of a group.
Start with simple questions with one-word answers. Move to more complex questions with longer answers.

○ Read out loud in class.

○ Take a video of your presentation at home.
Have the child film themself giving a presentation at home and then play it at school. Start by showing the video to the teacher, then a small group of peers, and then the whole class. Eventually have the child answer questions after sharing their video.

○ Talk during a group presentation.
Gradually increase both the size of the audience and the complexity of the child's participation.

○ Make a presentation.
Have the child create and deliver a presentation, first for a single peer, then a small group, and eventually the whole class or whole school.

Also: Mistakes, Perfectionism, Social Anxiety, Speaking

P

QUALIFIERS
See: Lying (inadvertent)

QUESTIONS
See: Making Decisions, Uncertainty

RAIN
See: Weather

REASSURANCE-SEEKING
Considerations
Reassurance-seeking and -giving is a healthy part of parent–child relationships, working to strengthen the parent–child bond while giving the child needed information and support. But reassurance-seeking becomes counterproductive when the child repeatedly asks the parent to guarantee that a feared outcome isn't going to happen. In these instances, it is as if there is a "right" answer, and only that answer will suffice. Definitive answers given in response to perseverative reassurance-seeking questions briefly calm the child while creating a problematic feedback loop that further fuels anxiety. Work with parents to provide emotional support without answering reassurance-seeking questions, helping the child learn to tolerate uncertainty.

See: Intrusive Thoughts, Uncertainty

RELIGIOUS THOUGHTS
See: Intrusive Thoughts, Perfectionism, Words and Phrases

REPEATING
See: Asymmetry, Checking, Just Right Feeling, Re-Reading

RE-READING
Considerations
Laborious re-reading often springs from the fear of inadvertently missing a word. This is different from anxiety about seeing a triggering word, or needing to go over a passage until the child has a "just right" feeling, both of which are covered elsewhere. The aim of these exposures is to resume more efficient reading, and to see that even if a word is missed, nothing terrible happens. Prior to starting exposures for re-reading, evaluate for dyslexia or other learning disabilities.

Exposures

- Cover each line after reading it.
  Have the child use their hand or a blank sheet of paper to cover all lines of text above the line they are reading so they can't be re-read.

- Read out loud without re-reading.

- Use your finger or a pencil to follow along while reading, keeping it moving.

- Read even though words are missing.
  Black out random words on a page. Have the child read, skipping the words that are missing.

Also: Just Right Feeling, Media, Words and Phrases

ROBBERS
See: Baddies, Navigating Home Alone

R

S

SAFETY

Considerations

Some children have intrusive thoughts about safety. They might worry about a range of mishaps including getting into an accident, a stove being left on, or home invasion. These intrusive thoughts often result in worry, reassurance-seeking, excessive checking, and avoidance. As always, exposure related to safety fears does not put the child in unsafe situations but instead gives them practice with the activities they are avoiding.

See: Checking, Fire, Hurting Oneself or Others, Intrusive Thoughts, Navigating Home Alone, Separation Anxiety, Uncertainty, Weather

SANTA

See: Costumed Characters

SCHOOL

Considerations

School refusal can be caused by a number of things, including anxiety, bullying, sensory issues, conflict at home, or learning disabilities. Therefore, it is important to understand the origins of the child's fear, and to implement multifaceted interventions as needed. While there is often great interest in getting the child back to school as soon as possible, it is best to use a step-by-step approach as detailed below.

Exposures

○ Look at the school website.

○ Ride by the school.

○ Play on the school playground.

○ Look at a yearbook or photos from school.
Talk with the child about their teacher and classmates.

○ Read books that take place at school.
Read a variety of books about school, focusing on the child's grade if possible.
Include positive, stressful, serious, and funny depictions of school.

○ Play **School** with puppets or dolls.

○ Imagine going to school.
Have an adult narrate the relevant aspects of going to school, starting with
the point at which the anxiety begins, be it getting ready, traveling to school,
or entering the building.

○ Go into the school building with someone.
Start with the least amount of support necessary for success, which might
mean walking the child to their desk, or bringing them to the front door to be
met by someone from school. Transition from a parent supporting the child,
to a staff member, to a friend. Gradually decrease support until the child is
entering school independently.

○ Spend more time at school.
Start with the length of time the child is able to tolerate. This might be 20
minutes, or one class period. Increase the amount of time spent at school
according to a schedule that has been planned in advance. Starting each class
with work the child finds easy may be helpful. Be mindful of the magnitude
and pacing of changes. So, for example, the schedule might include adding
20 minutes every fourth day, or an hour every other week. Avoid making
changes on Mondays, which are typically the hardest days for children anxious about school. Do not encourage, or even allow, the child to stay longer
than planned, even if they are doing well. Deviating from the plan damages
trust and is likely to sabotage future exposures. It is possible, however, to
collaboratively renegotiate the schedule, accelerating it if the child is handling re-entry well.

○ Move away from your parent at school.
Start with the parent in the classroom, if necessary, before having them
move into the hall or office. Once the parent is waiting in the parking lot,
add having them leave for short errands. Extend these errands until the
parent is away for the full school day.

S

○ Talk to a parent at scheduled times.
Schedule phone calls with the parent during the school day rather than allowing the child to call as needed. Reduce the number of these planned calls over time, then graduate to having the child listen to a recorded message rather than talking to the parent live.

○ Check in with a helper at school.
Create a schedule of check-ins to provide support at vulnerable times. As the situation begins to improve, there are two ways to reduce the number of check-ins. One is to allow the child to decide if they need a check-in, and to reward them for unused times. This works well for children who are able to identify how they are doing and what they need. The other option is for adults to determine when the child is ready to reduce the number of check-ins. This is useful for children who are less aware of what they need to remain regulated, who might skip a check-in to earn the reward but then go on to have a difficult day.

Also: Mistakes, Perfectionism, Separation Anxiety, Social Anxiety, Speaking

SELECTIVE EATING
Considerations
When working with a child with a limited palate, it is important to screen for oral motor or sensory processing differences, and to refer to a Speech and Language Pathologist or Occupational Therapist as needed. Digestive symptoms such as constipation or diarrhea should be evaluated by the child's doctor.

Even when supplementary services are needed, selective eating can be addressed with exposure. The goal is to support the child to tolerate being around non-preferred foods, interact with them, and eventually eat them. Some of the suggestions below are based on the concept of food chaining, which starts with an assessment of the child's current food repertoire, then introduces similar foods, and then pairs new foods with similar foods to increase the number of accepted foods. Typically, the same food needs to be presented repeatedly for change to occur. Keep in mind that asking a child to eat more than they are comfortable with is never helpful, and that children should not be pushed to the point of gagging.

Parents of selective eaters know how difficult and time consuming it is to change a child's eating habits. However, benefits to nutrition, energy level, emotional regulation, attention, health, and future wellness make it well worth the investment of time and energy.

S

Exposures

○ Make a collage using pictures of food.

○ Eat with a new food on the table.
Serve a non-preferred food alongside the child's preferred foods. Move from leaving the new food on a separate plate to putting a small portion on the child's plate. The child may eat the new food, or not, but should not be asked to do so.

○ Play with the new food.
Encourage the child to sculpt the new food, squish it, bend it, and make shapes out of it. Move from playing with the food with an implement, for example, raking mashed potatoes with a fork, to using hands. The purpose of this exposure is to play without any pressure to taste the new food.

○ Explore the new food.
Have the child begin by touching the new food. Progress through: smelling, licking, touching it to their teeth, and taking a tiny bite before taking a larger bite. Move slowly through this progression, performing each step with the same food many times over a number of meals before encouraging full-sized bites or shifting to a different new food.

○ Try new foods that are similar to foods you already like.
Have the parent present a non-preferred food prepared in a familiar way. For example, if the child eats mashed potatoes, try mashed cauliflower cooked and seasoned the same.

○ Help prepare a new food.

○ Combine new foods with foods you already eat.
For example, if the child already dips carrots in dressing, serve green peppers with the same dressing.

○ Eat different brands of your favorite foods.

○ Eat the new food first.
This exposure encourages the child to eat the non-preferred food while they are most hungry.

○ Drink less while eating.
Have the child reduce or eliminate drinking with meals so as to not fill up on fluids.

S

O Use the **Pass** system.
Pass tokens allow the child to opt out of eating a particular food as they
can trade in a token to say, "I pass." Gauge how many tokens the child will
need to start, reducing the number over time. The parent should continue
to serve what they would like to serve. Reward the child for unused tokens.

O Use the **No Thank You Bite**.
A No Thank You Bite means the child has to take one bite before declining a
food. Continue to serve foods to which the child has already said, "No thank
you," sticking with the rule that the child takes a single bite each time. The
wider the range of foods offered, the better.

Also: Contamination, Perfectionism, "Unhealthy" Foods, Vomiting

SELECTIVE MUTISM
See: Speaking, Social Anxiety

SEPARATION ANXIETY
Considerations
Separation anxiety typically manifests as avoidance of activities that require separation from the parent. Activities such as attending school, going to drop-off
birthday parties, falling asleep alone, and having the parent leave for work might
be met with excessive questions, tears, or refusal. While parents typically focus
on the inability to separate outside the home, evaluation often reveals difficulty
separating inside the home, too, with children unable to go into rooms or sleep
alone. To separate more successfully outside the home, children need ample practice separating in familiar environments. See Navigating Home Alone and Sleeping
Alone for ideas specific to those situations. As you are crafting exposure challenges
for separation anxiety, remember to focus on three things: the separation itself,
the feared consequence of the separation, and the withdrawal of safety behaviors.

Exposures

O Move away from your parent a little bit at a time.
If practicing in a therapy office, for example, move from having the parent
in the therapy room the whole time to having them step briefly into the hall,
then into the waiting room. After the parent is able to remain in the waiting
room, have them leave the building. Over the course of several sessions,
move from having the parent step outside, to sitting in the car, to driving

S

away and doing a quick errand. Picking up a treat for the child while the parent is gone is sure to sweeten the deal. A similar progression can be followed when visiting a relative, on a playdate, at swimming lessons, or at home.

○ Find something in a grocery store.
Have the parent choose an item for the child to find, starting with something that is midway down a grocery aisle. Aim for having the child leave the parent's side in every aisle. Over subsequent trips, increase the distance between parent and child within the same aisle. Older children can work up to going to a different aisle.

○ Play indoor **Hide and Seek**.
Take turns hiding and finding, with the adult hiding in increasingly difficult places. Expand the range of the game so the child is eventually moving further away from the parent.

○ Practice calm separations.
Roleplay upcoming events, such as basketball practice, a visit to the park, or a holiday party. Practice entering the venue, saying good-bye, and moving away from one another.

○ Stay inside while your parent goes outside.
Have the child play inside while a parent steps outside for short periods, such as to collect the mail or take out the trash. The child may need to start by watching from a window, moving away from the window over subsequent exposures. Have the child keep busy without a screen, which would be too distracting, working against the exposure.

○ Play outside while your parent stays inside.

○ Make good-byes short and sweet.

○ Call or text your parent less often, or not at all.
Systematically decrease the number of calls or texts allowed when the parent and child are apart, moving to no contact for routine separations. When the parent and child will be apart for longer stretches of time, schedule brief check-ins by phone or text rather than allowing the child to call when they feel anxious.

○ Play **Party Bingo**.
At a social event, have the child check off challenges to earn a prize. For example, they can: play with someone for 10 minutes, get a napkin from a different room, use the bathroom alone, get a plate of food, find the kitchen,

S

or learn the name of someone they don't know. Reward the completion of rows, and then the entire card.

○ Use a public restroom alone.
Begin by having the child go into the stall or cubicle while the parent waits near the sink or doorway. Move to having the parent wait outside the restroom.

○ Notice reassurance-seeking questions.
When faced with questions like, "When will you be back?," or "Will you be there to pick me up?" have the parent begin to identify, "That's a worry question" without answering it.

○ Leave your "safety items" at home.
Move away from "safety items" to bridge routine separations, including parental belongings, a particular water bottle, or a photo. Start by increasing the distance between the child and the object prior to having them leave it at home.

○ Put your fear into words.
Have the child say their fear out loud, for example, "My mom will go away and never come back," or "My dad will get into an accident and die." Help the child identify this as a worry thought rather than providing reassurance.

○ Imagine the situation you fear.
The therapist can narrate, for example, what would happen if a parent forgot to pick up the child after sports practice. Include what that would feel like, what would happen, who would be there to help, and what the child could do to help themself. When possible and within the bounds of safety, make the feared scenario happen, such as planning a late pick-up.

○ Play **1 Serious, 1 Silly**.
Take turns coming up with things that might happen while the parent is away. Alternate between realistic things like, "Mom could have to go to the hospital," and silly fates like, "Mom could get trapped in a giant bubble-gum bubble." Play the game first with the parent present, then in another room, then out of the house or office entirely. Some children might need to flip the order, starting with the parent out of the room and moving toward having them present. Do whichever is easiest first.

○ Spend the night at someone else's house.
Plan a sleepover, beginning with a house that is familiar to the child and

S

relatively nearby, such as a friend, babysitter, or grandparent. Move to sleepovers that are further away, with less familiar people, and covering longer stretches of time. Do not offer the option of coming home early but instead coach the adult in the household to support the child if anxiety strikes.

Also: Baddies, Intrusive Thoughts, Navigating Home Alone, School, Sleeping Alone, Uncertainty

SEX
See: Intrusive Thoughts

SHARKS
See: Dangerous Animals

SHOTS
See: Blood, Dentists, Doctors, Injections

SICKNESS
See: Health, "Unhealthy" Foods, Vomiting

SITUATIONAL MUTISM
See: Speaking, Social Anxiety

SLEEPING ALONE
Considerations
It's easy to fall into the habit of staying nearby as a child is falling asleep. Sometimes this is pleasant for everyone, in which case, there is no problem. But sometimes it takes an inordinate amount of time for the child to settle down, or there are tears and protests if the parent needs to step out. Children accustomed to having a parent sit with them often remain vigilant at bedtime, which is antithetical to relaxing and falling asleep. And children who do not fall asleep alone are more likely to have trouble sleeping through the night, waking and needing a parent to help them get back to sleep.

S

The first step, prior to starting exposure, is to establish a clear bedtime routine including one-on-one time with a parent. Bedtime should be the same every night, and often must be moved earlier as children who are overtired have more trouble winding down and falling asleep. It is also important to assess for fears of baddies, the dark, separation, or dying in the night. When other fears are found, start with exposures related to the core fear prior to addressing sleeping alone.

Exposures

○ Sleep with a parent nearby but not in your bed.
If the child is accustomed to having the parent sleep with them through the night, have the parent move to the floor or a nearby cot. Over time, the parent will move further across the room, into the hall, down the hall, and eventually back into their own room. If the child is accustomed to sleeping in the parent's bed, gradually move the child further away.

○ Fall asleep alone.
If the parent has been lying in bed as the child falls asleep, have the parent move from lying in bed, to sitting on the edge of the bed, to sitting nearby, and finally sitting across the room. Progress through this sequence fairly quickly. At every level, once good-night has been said, there is no more talking. If the child tries to engage, the parent can say, "It's time for sleep," or "We'll talk about that tomorrow," without responding to what the child has said. It's important for parents to be consistent here, remaining kind but firm about quieting down to sleep.

○ Take breaks from having a parent in the room.
Have the parent leave for brief periods of time while the child is falling asleep. After saying good-night, the parent can say, "I'll be back in a few minutes" and leave. This is not a trick; the parent is going to return. The parent, child, and therapist can work out the right starting point for how long the parent will be out of the room. For some children, this will be 20 seconds, for others, 2 or 3 minutes, or even 10 minutes. Whatever length of time has been agreed upon should be honored, with parents avoiding the temptation to stretch the time. Increase the time spent out of the room systematically. For example, you might add 2 minutes every fourth night, or 5 minutes each week. When the parent comes back into the room, they should stand briefly in the doorway. If the child is still awake, the parent can say, "Time for sleep. I'll be back in a few minutes" and leave again. This pattern continues until the child is asleep. If the child is clock-watching, turn or remove the clock.

S

○ Let your parent go back to their own activities at night.
Have the parent move further away after leaving the child's room. The parent might initially remain in the hall, then move to a nearby room, then further away, until the parent is able to be anywhere in the home. This is a planned exposure, which means that, up until the last step, the child will know where the parent is, but there should be no confirmation or additional reassurance about the parent's whereabouts.

○ Fall asleep without knowing exactly where your parent is.
Children often try to pin down their parents about where they will be going and what they will be doing when they leave the child's room. Have the parent move from answering these questions to saying something nonspecific like, "I'll be around," and eventually not answering the question at all.

○ Use a **Token System** for staying quietly in your room at night.
Start with three tokens a night. Have the parent take a token each time the child calls out or comes out of their room. Reward unused tokens in the morning, reinforcing the child for following the agreement. Decrease the number of tokens available to the child over time, or increase the number needed to earn a reward. This system can be used in combination with a schedule of timed checks on the child.

○ Stay in your own bed if you wake up at night.
Have the parent move from allowing the child to join them in bed to re-doing the final piece of the bedtime routine. For example, the parent might bring the child back to their room, say good-night in the usual way, leave briefly, and then return to check on them every 5 minutes until the child has fallen back to sleep. This will be exhausting, but if parents stick with it, it will eventually extinguish middle-of-the-night visits.

○ Let any adult who loves you put you to bed.
Sometimes, in two-parent households, children develop a preference about who puts them to bed. To help them develop flexibility about this, they may need to start with both parents putting them to bed at the same time. Then have the "preferred" parent step out of the room briefly during the nighttime routine. Work toward alternating which parent puts the child to sleep. Once the child has mastered being put to bed by either parent, have the "preferred" parent stay out past the child's bedtime. The family can also work toward both parents being out so the child can be put to bed by a grandparent or sitter.

Also: Baddies, Dark, Health, Intrusive Thoughts, Navigating Home Alone, Uncertainty

S

SMALL SPACES

See: Confined Spaces

SNAKES

See: Dangerous Animals

SOCIAL ANXIETY

Considerations

At the heart of social anxiety is the fear of embarrassment. Children with social anxiety are afraid of looking ignorant or silly. They worry about being reprimanded or having people laugh at them. Despite being social, they shy away from being in the spotlight. It is not unusual to see angry outbursts following unwanted attention such as having their picture taken or getting hurt. Exposure for social anxiety focuses on activities that bring attention to the self, which often include risking looking foolish or being told no.

Exposures

○ Tell an embarrassing story.
   Take turns telling stories. Start with fictional stories, then something embarrassing that happened to someone else, and finally, something embarrassing that happened to the storyteller.

○ Walk around a busy place.
   Have the child move from no eye contact, to eye contact, to smiling. Set challenges such as: look at four people, or get someone to smile back at you.

○ Wave to strangers from the car.

○ Talk to a classmate you don't know well.
   Help the child plan a friendly question in advance, such as, "Where did you get that shirt? It's cool." Move to other conversation starters such as, "Do you have any pets?" Phase out the planning while maintaining goals like talking to someone at lunch or inviting someone to play at recess.

○ Ask people questions.
   Have the child start with something expected, such as, "Can you tell me where the bathroom is?" Then have them move to nonsensical questions like, "Do you sell elephants here?" in a pet store, or "Have you ever been to the

S

moon?" to a neighbor, remembering that the goal is to evoke, and survive, mild embarrassment. Some children find this easier to do with familiar people and some with less familiar people. Start wherever the child is more comfortable.

○ Ask a question in class.
Have the child start with a genuine question, then ask a question the teacher has already answered or a question others will see as odd.

○ Wear clothing that stands out.
Help the child choose a bright color, something mismatched, or a shirt that says, "Ask me a question," with the intention of drawing attention to themselves. Move from wearing the clothing for a brief time in an easy place to longer stretches in harder spots. For example, the child might wear the clothing first at home, then on an errand, and finally at school.

○ Answer questions in class.
There are several ways to manipulate the difficulty of this exposure. One is to move from having the teacher give the child notice about the question ahead of time to asking spontaneously. Another is to move from brief, factual answers to more complex or opinion-based answers. And a third is to have the child move from giving correct answers to answering incorrectly on purpose.

○ Do something surprising that other people will notice.
Consider having an adult do these activities near the child first. Start small, such as by dropping something. Move to less socially acceptable activities such as burping, speaking too loudly, or walking to the front of a line.

○ Sign up for a new activity.
Have the child start a sport, take a class, or join a club that will put them with a group of people they don't already know.

○ Say "Yes" to invitations.
Have the child accept any social invitations they receive, whether they want to go or not.

○ Give a speech or play an instrument in public.

○ Play **Rock Paper Scissors** or another game with someone you don't know well.

S

○ Eat alone at lunch.
Or, if eating alone is comfortable, have the child eat with people they don't know well.

○ Order something not on the menu, or ask to have something changed.
An adult might model this first by asking, for example, if the restaurant serves a particular kind of tea, or to have their sandwich cut in three pieces. Over subsequent restaurant visits, have the child be the one to make the special request.

○ **Collect No's.**
Create a list of requests that will likely be rejected, for example, "Can I see the storeroom?" in a store, or "Can I have your backpack?" to a classmate. Challenge the child to ask these questions, with the goal of getting as many "No" answers as possible.

Also: Mistakes, Perfectionism, Speaking, Uncertainty

SPEAKING
Considerations

This category refers to children who are fully able to speak in some settings, but do not speak in all settings. Diagnostically, this is called Selective Mutism or Situational Mutism, the treatment for which is multifaceted. Referral for evaluation by a Speech and Language Pathologist can help determine if there are speech-related concerns such as difficulty with receptive or expressive language skills. Once that has been ruled out, assess the child's speech repertoire. In what settings are they speaking and not speaking? In whose company do they speak? What kinds of communication do they employ? Do they use gestures, vocalizations, or fully spoken sentences? Do they initiate as well as respond?

When it comes time to craft an exposure hierarchy, remember it is typically easier for the child to read or speak others' words than their own words. It may be easier to give factual answers than their own opinions. The easiest questions to answer will be Yes/No questions, followed by multiple choice, and finally open-ended questions. It may be easier to speak in a place the child has never been, versus a place the child has already been silent.

Treatment for Selective Mutism involves frequent mini exposures with just one variable changing at a time. For example, if the child is not communicating at all, start with a highly engaging activity the child can take part in using nods or hand gestures. If they already use gestures, try a game that involves making

S

animal noises. If they do not talk in front of the teacher in the classroom, start with the teacher in another room or outside, then in the classroom with their back turned, and eventually facing the child.

Addressing parental accommodation is also critical. Support the parent to treat the child as though they are a talker. Help them make room for the child to speak without putting pressure on them. Help parents see where they are speaking for the child, and ask them to wait a little longer before jumping in.

Exposures

○ Play games using sounds.
For example, play **Animal Go Fish** by asking for a card with the appropriate animal sound. Play **Battleship** by pointing to a letter and then clicking your tongue a certain number of times to guess the ship's location.

○ Keep time with a song.
Begin by offering something to make music with, such as a pencil to hit against a desk. Move to using body parts, like clapping hands in time with the music or clicking your tongue. Then try humming.

○ Make noises while playing.
Have the child move from nonvocal to vocal sound effects, such as car noises, crashes, animal sounds, and hums. The therapist can make all these sounds, too.

○ Say "Yes" and "No" without words.
Work out a system for indicating yes, no, and I don't know. Progress from nonverbal, to vocal, to verbal responses.

○ Use gestures.
Support the child to use nonverbal communication in increasingly sophisticated ways, for example adding facial expressions to pointing to help convey meaning.

○ Order food at a restaurant.
Begin by having the child point to their selection on a menu. Move to having them tell the parent what they want in front of the waitperson. End by having the child speak to the server directly.

○ Make a recording to share.
Record the child speaking, starting with reading or answering simple questions posed by a support person. Over time, work toward more creative,

S

impromptu speech. Plan to share the recording with someone to whom the child does not normally speak. Initially have the person listen alone, then move to having the person listen with the child present.

○ Play **School** or **Birthday Party**.
Vary the play to include scenarios, people, or environments where the child does not currently speak.

○ Practice a conversation in advance.
Roleplay conversations that might happen in public, helping the child practice verbal responses.

○ Pay for something at a store.

○ Ask a librarian for a book.

○ Say hello to someone.
Move the child from smiling or waving to verbally greeting. Have them practice both responding to and initiating greetings, moving from known to unknown people, and from peers to adults, going from easier to harder each time.

○ Speak to your parent in front of someone.
Move the child from speaking in front of an unknown person to a known person, and from speaking in front of a child to an adult, going from easier to harder each time.

○ Speak in a classroom.
Begin in an empty classroom with only a support person present. Gradually add other people including the teacher and classmates, moving from friends to less-known peers.

○ Participate in something fun.
Think of places and activities that will provide the opportunity to speak to a variety of people. Have the child help at a booth at a fair, hand out fliers, or greet people at church.

○ Give one-word answers to questions.
Start with preplanned questions and responses before moving to unplanned questions and responses. Move from factual questions to opinions. For example, from "What do you call a baby cat?" to "What's your favorite color?"

○ Give longer answers to questions.

S

○ Do a **Curiosity Scavenger Hunt** or play **Getting to Know You Bingo**.
For example: Find someone in your class who: has a pet, likes math, has a sister, or plays soccer.

○ Notch up the volume.
Have the child experiment with turning up the volume on a video to develop a number scale going from 0, meaning you can't hear it at all, to 5, a comfortable volume. Begin using this number scale to encourage audible speech, saying things along the lines of, "That's a 2. My ears need a 3. Can you help me out?"

○ Speak into a microphone.
Move from having the microphone off to turning it on, and from speaking in private to in front of other people.

○ Sing karaoke.

Also: Mistakes, Perfectionism, Public Speaking, Social Anxiety

SPIDERS
See: Bugs

STAINS
See: Contamination, Perfectionism

STAIRS
See: Navigating Home Alone

STINGING INSECTS
See: Bees

STORMS
See: Noises, Weather

S

STRANGERS
See: Baddies, Crowded Places, Differentness, Separation Anxiety, Social Anxiety, Speaking

SUICIDE (FEAR OF DYING BY)
See: Hurting Oneself or Others, Intrusive Thoughts, Uncertainty

SURROUNDED
See: Crowded Places, Noises, Social Anxiety

SWALLOWING
See: Choking, Medicine

SWIMMING
See: Trying New Things, Water Immersion

SYMMETRY
See: Asymmetry

S

TALKING
See: Speaking

TEENAGERS
See: Differentness, Growing Up

TERRORISTS
See: Baddies

TESTS
Considerations
Because children develop test anxiety for a variety of reasons, it is important to determine the root cause before beginning treatment. Sometimes test anxiety arises out of the child's difficulty tolerating mistakes. They might strive for perfection, making test-taking extremely stressful. Other children develop test anxiety due to an inaccurate assessment of their ability coupled with low self-esteem. Children in need of academic support for learning disabilities may fear tests as yet another demonstration of their perceived inadequacy. It is important to do the detective work of figuring out what is causing the stress, and then craft an individualized plan.

See: Mistakes, Perfectionism, School, Timed Activities, Uncertainty

THROWING UP
See: Vomiting

THUNDER
See: Noises, Weather

TIGHT SPACES
See: Confined Spaces

TIMED ACTIVITIES
Considerations
When a child presents with anxiety about timed activities, it is important to rule out difficulty with processing speed or visual tracking. If present, ensure that the child is receiving treatment and support for these concerns prior to addressing the anxiety. Once exposure to timed activities begins, proceed at a pace that allows the child to successfully complete activities before presenting harder challenges. Exposure must also include challenges that stretch the limits of the child's abilities and confidence, as part of what we are doing is helping the child learn to tolerate and accept uncertainty and imperfection.

Exposures

○ Do an activity with a timer running in the background.
  Begin with fun activities that are not typically timed, periodically stopping and restarting the timer. Move to activities in which time matters.

○ Use timers in games you already play.
  For example, use a timer to count down the start of **Hide and Seek**. When playing board games, set challenges such as getting to a certain spot before the timer goes off.

○ Play board games that use a timer, such as **The 5-Second Rule**, **Perfection**, **Boggle**, or **Scattergories**.

○ Do a **Beat the Clock** challenge.
  Most children's party games can be converted to timed activities.

○ Use a timer to see who can do a chore fastest, or try to better your own time.

○ Play **Alphabet** with a timer.
  Work together to find animals that start with every letter of the alphabet, or foods, or use another category of the child's choosing. Move toward making

T

the game competitive, challenging the child to finish ahead of the adult or to complete the game with the fewest letters skipped.

○ Set a timer during homework.
Have the child practice doing homework with a timer, first by setting but not attending to it, then by completing an individual assignment within a certain amount of time.

Also: Mistakes, Perfectionism, Social Anxiety, Uncertainty

TOADS
See: Frogs

TOILETING
Considerations
Exposure is appropriate when it is clear that the child is aware of the urge to urinate or defecate and has sufficient control of their body but is resistant to, or afraid of, using the toilet. First experiment with a variety of toilets including a potty seat, a squatty-potty, and the regular toilet with a footstool. It is easier for children to use the toilet when their feet are grounded and the opening is correctly sized, which might mean adding an insert or special seat. Note that it is harder to withhold bowel movements when sitting, so children of all genders might be encouraged to squat or sit but not stand, even when urinating.

Prior to starting exposure related to toileting, it is important to rule out constipation, which is a chicken-or-egg problem. Children who are constipated avoid moving their bowels because it hurts, and children who avoid moving their bowels get constipated. Unrecognized food sensitivities and autoimmune issues can lead to constipation, as well. Whatever the cause, constipation needs to be treated prior to, or along with, exposure for resistance to using the toilet. Remember that children experience shame when they struggle to achieve important milestones. Normalize the trouble they are having, and be sure to recognize the achievement when they reach their goals. Print a certificate, have a dance party, or craft a poop trophy!

Exposures

○ Be in the room with other people as they use the toilet.
Normalize toileting by having the child see other family members using

T

the toilet. Sometimes a visit with cousins who use the toilet is all it takes to get toileting on track.

- O Read books about toileting.

- O Draw people toileting.

- O Have dolls or stuffed animals use the toilet.

- O Do diaper or underwear changes only in the bathroom.

- O Do all peeing and pooping in the bathroom.
  If the child is using a potty seat, have the family leave it in the bathroom. If the child is eliminating in diapers, pull-ups, or underwear, have the parent prompt them to go into the bathroom if they see signs that the child needs to, or is, peeing or pooping.

- O Sit on the toilet or potty seat.
  The child may need to start fully clothed and move to sitting in a diaper or underwear before they are able to sit bare-bottomed. They may also need to begin with a quick touch down, gradually adding time until they are sitting on the toilet for a full 3 minutes.

- O Pour pretend pee into the toilet.
  Have the child sit on the toilet or potty seat, spread their legs, and pour water from a small cup into the toilet to simulate urinating.

- O Drop pretend poop in the toilet.
  Have the child sit on the toilet or potty seat and drop small bits of soft food into the toilet to simulate pooping. Rolled-up pieces of bread work well for this, starting with very small pieces and moving to larger clumps.

- O Stay in the room while someone else flushes the toilet.

- O Flush the toilet with the lid down, then up.

- O Do **Sit Time**.
  Help the family choose four or five times a day to go into the bathroom for Sit Time, which is 2 or 3 minutes of sitting on the toilet or potty seat. Pick typical toileting times such as immediately after getting out of bed, before leaving for school, after lunch, after dinner, and before bed. Sit Time may need to start clothed, working toward bare-bottomed. The child may continue to pee or poop in a diaper or underwear, but often functional toileting begins during Sit Time. Do not make Sit Time longer than a few minutes, and do not encourage strenuous pushing during this time.

T

○ Put pee and poop in the toilet.
If the child pees or poops in their underwear or diaper, have them transfer it into the toilet before washing or disposing. This is not a punishment; it's a matter-of-fact statement that pee and poop belong in the toilet. The yuck factor increases motivation to reach the goal of age-appropriate toileting. This intervention, however, must be delivered supportively. For example, the parent might say, "I know it's yucky. It's going to be so nice to not have to do this anymore."

○ Sit on the toilet to poop or pee if using a diaper.
Have the child sit on the toilet in their diaper to pee or poop. Start by cutting a small hole in the diaper, then make it larger and larger until the poop falls into the toilet. If the child is dependent on the feel of a snug diaper, they may need the legs of the diaper to be gradually cut, making it looser over time.

Also: Contamination, Wiping

TORNADOES
See: Weather

TRAVELING
Considerations
Some children routinely experience distress while traveling. Being out of the usual routine can be highly disconcerting, especially when regular meals and bedtime are abandoned. Sometimes apprehension has to do with the fear of being separated from a parent, or difficulty being in crowds. Trouble with visual or auditory processing can be a complicating variable, and difficulty with motor skills can make navigating unfamiliar terrain scary. Careful assessment will determine if referral to another provider, such as an Occupational Therapist, is needed, and if exposure is appropriate. Once you have an understanding of what is driving the child's fear, the following sections may be helpful.

See: Change in Plans, Confined Spaces, Crowded Places, Flying, Selective Eating, Separation Anxiety, Trying New Things

T

TREATMENT AVOIDANCE

Considerations

Starting therapy can be frightening for children as it involves sharing vulner-abilities with a stranger. The child has no way of knowing how the therapist will respond, and if they will be punished or made to feel bad about themself. It is the therapist's duty to win the trust of the child, knowing that until trust is in place, the child is likely to avoid treatment with an array of tactics, from running away, to not talking, to being silly or changing the subject.

Children often need help acclimating to the therapist and therapy room prior to engaging in the work of therapy. As with all exposure, it is best to work collaboratively with the child to figure out how much talk therapy they are able to do. During these exposures, if the child becomes silly or walks away, recognize this as an attempt at self-regulation. Allow the child to regulate, assisting them if needed, prior to returning to work.

Exposures

○ Look at pictures of the therapist's office.
  Before starting treatment, send the child a digital file with a letter saying you are looking forward to meeting them. Include pictures of yourself and the office. Encourage the family to preview therapy by looking at the pictures beforehand, and to continue to review them even after therapy has begun.

○ Share your interests with your therapist.
  Begin sessions by talking about topics of interest to the child or engaging in preferred activities. In play-based therapies, invite the child to bring their own toys to share. Print coloring pages of favorite activities, stories, or characters.

○ Take turns deciding what to do.

○ Talk about therapy at home.
  Have the parent talk about the therapist and therapy in positive ways between sessions.

○ Have fun starting and stopping therapy sessions.
  Create a ritual for starting and stopping sessions. For example, you might begin with a meditation, emotional check-in, or intention setting. You could start with the "best thing" and "worst thing" of the week, or each pull a get-ting-to-know-you question from a question jar. Pay equal attention to ending the session, perhaps with a unique handshake or a consistent well-wishing statement as you say good-bye.

T

○ Give therapy and your therapist a chance.

Also: Feelings, Mistakes, Perfectionism, Separation Anxiety, Speaking

TRIGGERING WORDS OR PHRASES
See: Words and Phrases

TRYING NEW THINGS
Considerations
When a child is reluctant to try new things, it's important to create an exposure plan that includes both intentional and natural exposures. For example, one part of the plan may be to set up a hierarchy of intentional exposures to increase the child's participation in and skills related to a new hobby. Another part of the exposure plan might be to create a family culture of appreciation for novelty. Encourage the family to keep an eye out for all sorts of novel experiences, from trying a new food to playing with a new friend. Over time, the child will learn to recognize that apprehension is an invitation to try something new. Keep in mind that difficulty with visual processing or motor planning can make children anxious about being in new environments, and refer for evaluation as needed.

Exposures

○ Write a **New Things I Tried** list.
  This list will chronicle new experiences such as foods, activities, and books. Set goals for adding to the list. The child may enjoy getting a new journal for this or decorating the cover of a plain notebook.

○ Create a **New Things Relay Race**.
  The whole family can participate in this activity together. Draw a map of a race route with blank squares. When someone has a new experience, they get to write it in one of the blocks. Each family member can fill in their own section, or the race can be done cooperatively to earn a prize at the end.

○ Learn about new activities in advance.
  Preview what the child is likely to experience. Look up the venue online, watch videos, or look at pictures. Whenever possible, connect the new experience to something the child has done before.

○ Make a timeline of how the new activity will go.

T

○ Use the **3 Steps to New Things**.
Teach the child the following progression: Step 1) Learn about the new thing ahead of time, Step 2) Watch it from the sidelines, Step 3) Join in. Support the child with statements such as, "We're on Step 1, we're just learning about it," or "You're on Step 2, you're watching."

○ Create a **New Things Challenge Jar**
Work with the child to write a variety of new activities on slips of paper and place them in the jar. Decide on a number of new activities per day or week. Each day or week, have the child draw the requisite number of slips and do the activities. The goal is to have the child habituate to uncertainty by having the repeated experience of feeling apprehensive, doing the new thing anyway, and having it work out fine.

New Things Challenge Jar
✔ Eat a food you've never eaten.
✔ Read a book you've never read.
✔ Watch a show you've never heard of.
✔ Play a game you've never played.
✔ Combine two foods that aren't usually eaten together.
✔ Try a new sport.
✔ Go to a new friend's house.
✔ Speak to a new person.
✔ Wear a new piece of clothing.
✔ Try a different brand of food.
✔ Plan a family outing somewhere new.

○ Make a routine of trying new things.
Encourage the family to incorporate new things into their routine. They might enjoy New Food Tuesdays or New Movie Fridays.

○ Do new activities on your own.
Have the parent withdraw accommodations that protect the child from new experiences. If they are apprehensive talking to strangers, for example, have the parent stop ordering for the child at a restaurant. If they only take part in activities when the parent stays, have them go with a friend, instead.

Also: Change in Plans, Losing, Mistakes, Separation Anxiety, Uncertainty

T

UNCERTAINTY

Considerations

Anxiety craves certainty, which is why excessive reassurance-seeking is nearly ubiquitous for anxious children. ERP aimed at helping children learn to tolerate uncertainty is often needed to supplement other forms of exposure. Without it, you will see a snowballing effect of repeated reassurance leading to an increase in anxiety. To get out of this unproductive loop, therapists will need to teach parents to tolerate their child's distress rather than trying to alleviate it. The aim is to have parents calmly and empathically say, "It's hard not to know for sure," or "Your worry wants you to be sure, but it's okay to not know," and then not answer the reassurance-seeking question.

Exposures

○ Practice feeling unsure.

Have the parent answer reassurance-seeking questions honestly the first time they come up. For example, the parent might say, "There's no rain in the forecast today," if the child is asking an anxious question about the weather. If the question is asked again, the parent can say, "I already answered that." And the third time, "I'm going to help you by not answering your worry questions anymore." Once the child is familiar with this process, the parent can move to, "That's a worry question. Answering feeds worry, so I'm not going to answer that question."

○ Look for the truth.

Teach parents to shift from providing definitive answers, such as promising a bad thing isn't going to happen, to giving qualified answers such as, "As far as I know, you aren't going to throw up today," or "I have no reason to think there's a bad guy upstairs."

○ See how many **Question Cards** you can save.
Have the parent give the child three pieces of paper to serve as Question Cards. The cards can be decorated with question marks or pictures of favorite foods to remind the child that reassurance "feeds" worry. It's the child's job to keep as many cards as possible over the course of the day. If the child asks a worry question, the parent is to say, "That would be a card" rather than answering the question. If the child feels that they must have the question answered, they can go find their cards and give one to the parent, who will then answer the question realistically, without reassurance. The child has three cards to spend over the course of the day, and will be rewarded for unused cards. When the parent says, "That would be a card," the child can opt to say, "Never mind," in which case, no question is answered and no card is lost. If the child uses all three cards and then asks another worry question, the parent is to say, "I'm sorry, you're out of cards," and then not answer the question. Teach parents to remain empathic, even if the child melts down, without providing reassurance about the worry. Develop a menu of rewards for unused cards.

○ Learn to spot reassurance-seeking questions.
Have the parent begin to identify, "That's a worry question" rather than answering. Children often seek confirmation in more subtle ways, saying things like, "I'm not going to choke, right?" Teach parents and children to be on the lookout for all forms of reassurance-seeking and -giving.

○ Say your fear out loud.
Using the child's own words, turn each worry question into a statement such as, "I might stop breathing in the night," or "A kidnapper could be hiding upstairs." Have the child make these statements without undoing them or securing reassurance afterward.

○ Record the fear.
Coach the child to write what they fear, then record themself speaking "with feeling." Have the child listen to the recording on a loop, increasing the time spent listening. Move from listening with a support person to listening alone, and from listening with a mild distraction to listening without distraction. After a period of time, move to listening while doing an activity the child avoids, such as going upstairs alone, eating, or sitting near a knife.

Also: Every entry in this book! Trouble tolerating uncertainty contributes to virtually every fear.

U

UNFAIRNESS
Considerations

It is natural to compare oneself to others, and developmentally typical for children to be concerned about fairness. Problems arise, however, when a child becomes preoccupied with comparisons, looking at their siblings or peers, seeing differential treatment, and getting stuck or melting down.

It is not unusual for parents to inadvertently complicate the matter by trying to convince their child that whatever is happening is, in fact, fair. Or they bend over backward to keep everything equal, which typically backfires, too.

An important first step is to acknowledge the difference the child is perceiving, and to validate their feelings about it, "You wish you had the same bedtime as your brother," or "It makes you sad that your sister got invited to her friend's party. You wish you had a special place to go." Empathy goes a long way toward helping the child feel heard, opening them up to learning about the greater good while teaching the difference between fair and equal.

Screen for trauma, loss, and ASD in children who are preoccupied with or rigid about fairness.

Exposures

○ Take turns dividing things.
  In homes with multiple children, it can be helpful to take turns dividing things such as cutting cake, pouring cereal, or handing out craft supplies. Develop a system for taking turns, or flip a coin to decide who will do what.

○ Read books about unfairness.

○ Talk about a time something happened that was unfair.
  Debrief following experiences the child sees as unfair. Talk about how they were handled by the child and the adult. Ask what the child thinks could have been done differently.

○ Volunteer as a family to do something that helps other people.

○ Chip in by doing chores.
  Have the parent rotate chores among family members. Make sure the child has the experience of cleaning up someone else's mess and the experience of someone doing something helpful for them. Emphasize how each person's chores contribute to the whole family.

U

○ Practice solving problems with other people.
Teach the child to work out their own conflicts by expressing themself calmly, compromising, creating contracts, and using chance.

○ Use dice or spinners to randomly decide things.
Dice and spinners can be used to determine how many cookies, handfuls of popcorn, or pieces of paper a child gets. They can also be used to determine who gets a preferred seat, to go first, or to pick a show.

○ Learn to accept differences in privileges and responsibilities.
In homes with multiple children, have the parent align privileges and responsibilities with each child's age and maturity level, as opposed to all children having identical privileges and responsibilities.

Also: Change in Plans, Interruption, Losing

"UNHEALTHY" FOODS

Considerations

Some children develop extreme concerns about whether the food they are eating is "healthy," with a level of anxiety far surpassing appropriate nutritional awareness. Children might worry about food causing a specific condition, illness, or disease. For example, a child might avoid all sugar for fear of developing diabetes. Other children present with a more generalized fear of food being "unhealthy." Extreme concern about food is often seen in the context of OCD, and can be accompanied by excessive reassurance-seeking and rigid, rule-based eating.

In terms of differential diagnosis, fear of "unhealthy" foods is different from the restrictive eating patterns that are characteristic of anorexia. Children with a fear of "unhealthy" foods do not avoid food for the purpose of losing weight. They do not have unrealistic views about the size of their body. This fear is also different from selective eating, which causes children to avoid certain foods due to texture or previous experience, not based on perceived healthiness.

Exposures

○ Make a list of foods that make you nervous.
Work with the child to make a list of foods that concern them. Help them identify which are "sometimes foods" to eat in moderation and which are "anytime foods" to eat more regularly. After the list is made, coach parents to stop answering questions about the healthiness of these foods.

U

○ Use a **Token System** to help you ask fewer questions.
The purpose of the Token System is to reduce food-related reassurance-seeking. Start with three tokens a day. Each time a reassurance-seeking question about food is asked, the parent is to say, "That would be a token." The child then has a choice. They can give up a token to have the parent answer the question, or they can say, "Never mind." If the question doesn't get answered, the child keeps the token, and also eats the food they've asked about. If they don't eat the food, they lose the token. Unused tokens turn into points that can be cashed in for rewards. If the child uses all three tokens and asks another food-related question, the parent is to say, "I'm sorry, you're out of tokens," and not answer the question. The use of physical tokens is important as it requires the child to retrieve one and hand it to the parent, breaking up the automaticity of asking and answering these questions. The number of tokens available to the child should be reduced over time. Additionally, parents can be coached to give less definitive answers even after the child has given them a token.

○ Take steps toward eating food that seems scary.
Start by placing the target food on the child's plate. Over subsequent exposures, move to having the child poke it, smell it, lick it, touch it to their teeth, then take a tiny bite, then a larger bite. Be sure to maintain a neutral stance, without reassurance.

○ Eat mixed-up meals.
Have the parent serve food at atypical times, such as breakfast food for dinner or dinner food at snack-time.

○ Eat a backward meal, with dessert first.

○ Stop checking labels.
If needed, have the parent black out dates or transfer food to generic containers to prevent the child from checking labels for things like portion size or nutrition information.

Also: Contamination, Selective Eating, Uncertainty, Vomiting

UPSTAIRS
See: Navigating Home Alone

U

URBAN LEGENDS
See: Baddies

URINATING
See: Toileting, Wiping

U

VACUUM CLEANER
See: Noises

VAMPIRES
See: Baddies

VEGETABLES
See: Selective Eating

VOMITING
Considerations
Although parents are often surprised to hear this, the fear of vomiting, also called emetophobia, is one of the most common childhood fears. Prior to treating emetophobia with exposure, it is important to rule out gastrointestinal (GI) concerns including reflux, and to consider testing for illnesses such as strep.

Children with emetophobia typically avoid everything that reminds them of prior episodes of vomiting. It is not unusual to see an adamant refusal to go certain places, wear certain clothing, or eat certain foods based on the mistaken notion that all are somehow dangerous and will cause vomiting again. Children with emetophobia studiously avoid people who have been sick and things linked, in the child's mind, with those people. Exposure aims to trigger apprehension about throwing up. We want to get the child thinking about vomiting, and to remove reassurances that it won't happen. Pay careful attention to safety behaviors as you begin exposure for emetophobia as they will render the challenges ineffective.

Exposures

○ Say *vomit* or words like it repeatedly.
Have the child play with the word by saying it fast or slow, in funny voices or accents, loudly or quietly.

○ Make a list of vomit words.
The list could include: barf, spew, puke, hurl, expel, upchuck, rainbow burp, yack, retch, purge, gag, chunder, toss your cookies, and spurt. Do an online search; there are literally hundreds of synonyms for throwing up. Review the list with the child to find the funniest, most disgusting, most common, and most confusing words and phrases. Keep the list nearby as you will use it for many of these exposures.

○ Do a **Word Search** looking for words that remind you of throwing up.
There are websites that will create a Word Search for you after you enter relevant keywords such as: vomit, smelly, sick, disgusting, chunky, and spew.

○ Play **Vomit Go Fish**.
Write a vomit synonym on each of four index cards until you have a total of 52 cards. Shuffle and deal the cards, then take turns asking, for example, "Do you have a hurl?," or "Do you have an upchuck?"

○ Write and decorate the word *vomit*.
Have the child write vomit words in block letters and decorate them. Hang this vomit "art" in prominent places.

○ Play **Vomit Frisbee** and **Find It** with fake vomit.

○ Look at pictures of vomit.
Prescreen the photos to adjust the level of grossness.

○ Draw on pictures of vomit.
Find pictures of vomit online and print them out. Work with the child to turn a pool of vomit into a lake scene, for example, with boats and people swimming in it, or a scoop of ice cream atop a cone. Be creative.

○ Look at photos of vomit and try to guess what the person who threw up had eaten.

○ Draw vomit and people vomiting.

○ Have a **Pretend Vomiting Contest**.
Act out vomiting in increasingly realistic ways, including doubling over,

running to the bathroom, and eventually having the child fill their mouth and "vomit" into the toilet.

○ Listen to vomit noises.
Vomit sounds can be found on YouTube or streaming services, or you can create them. Have the child listen without the visuals, increasing the volume over time.

○ Make pretend vomit.
Aim for a concoction that looks and smells real. Move from having the child look at the mixture, to smelling it, to pouring it into the toilet while simulating vomiting. Using a less-foul mixture, have the child fill their mouth and spit the fake vomit into the toilet.

○ Watch videos of throwing up.
Move from animals, to babies, to small children, to older children, to teens and adults. Begin with the sound off if necessary, then increase the volume over time. There are a wealth of vomit videos online, from funny to truly disgusting. Prescreen videos ahead of time.

○ Describe in detail what it feels like to vomit.

○ Do a vomit puzzle.
Believe it or not, there are vomit puzzles out there. Or you can make one by printing out an image of vomit and cutting it into pieces for the child to assemble.

○ Make a video of yourself pretending to vomit.
Have the child fill their mouth with something like minestrone soup, and spit it into the toilet. Encourage them to make it realistic. Watch the video forward and backward.

Basic Vomit Recipe
1. Chew up some light-colored crackers or biscuits
2. Spit them into a bowl or bag
3. Add water, apple juice, or vinegar (just a little)
4. Mash it up
5. Add partially chewed vegetables to make the mixture chunky

Alternate Vomit Recipe
1. Crush crackers in a bowl
2. Add oatmeal and a bit of water
3. Microwave the mixture for 30 seconds
4. Drain off any extra water
5. Add corn or chewed-up carrots
6. Add a spoonful of honey or syrup

Add-Ins to Up the Ick Factor
✓ Oatmeal
✓ Gelatin
✓ Flaked cereal
✓ Granola
✓ Small pieces of fruit or vegetables
✓ Bread
✓ Mashed beans
✓ Raisins
✓ Milk
✓ Orange juice
✓ Pickle relish
✓ Sour cream
✓ String cheese

○ Interact with clothing that makes you think about vomiting.
Have the child move from being in the same room with the clothing, to touching it, to putting it on and immediately taking it off, to wearing it in a more sustained way.

○ Go back to eating foods that make you think about vomiting.
Work with the child to create a list of foods they associate with vomiting. Targeting one food at a time, begin by putting the food on the table while the child is eating. Later put it on the child's plate without the expectation that they will eat it. Move to eating a single bite of the food, and finally a full serving of it. If the child needs smaller steps, start with a different brand of the target food, moving toward the very same food purchased from the same store or restaurant.

○ Listen to the truth.
Children who are afraid of vomiting want their parents to guarantee that it isn't going to happen. Teach parents to instead say, "I have no reason to think you are going to get sick," or "I don't know," rather than giving guarantees about not getting sick.

○ Play a computer or video game that involves vomit.

○ Be honest with yourself about the possibility of getting sick.
Have the child practice saying, "I might get sick," "Someday I'm going to throw up," "It's always possible that this will make me sick," and other sentences suggesting that vomiting could, and probably will, happen someday.

○ Make yourself burp.
As you may know, this can be done by swallowing air and then bringing it back up, or drinking something carbonated. For greater difficulty, have the child say, "I'm going to puke" while burping.

○ Make yourself feel nauseous on purpose.
Have the child eat something that sits heavily in the stomach, smell spoiled food, or read a book in the car to purposely induce nausea.

Also: Contamination, Dizziness, Health, Panic, Selective Eating, Uncertainty, "Unhealthy" Foods, Words and Phrases

v

WASPS
See: Bees

WATER IMMERSION
Considerations
When children are afraid of water, it is important to rule out a sensory processing disorder, particularly difficulty with vestibular processing. Some children with sensory processing disorders feel like they don't know which end is up when they are in the water, whereas others have the opposite experience, recognizing for the first time where all their body parts are.

Exposures

○ Go to a place that has water.
 Have the family visit water in the community, be it a creek, river, lake, or the ocean.

○ Go outside in the rain.

○ Play in a sprinkler.

○ Wear goggles in the bath or shower.

○ Put your hand above a drain.
 Fill a sink, then open the drain and have the child put their fingers increasingly close to the drain as the water swirls around it.

○ Spray water on your face.
 Using a mister, have the child gently spray water on their face. Start by covering eyes with goggles, hands, or a washcloth if necessary, moving to having the child simply squeeze their eyes shut.

○ Go on a boat ride.

○ Let someone wash your hair.
Move from allowing the child to wear goggles, to using a washcloth to cover their eyes, to using a hand, to keeping their eyes closed on their own. Having the child tilt their head back will be easier than tucking their chin.

○ Blow bubbles underwater.
Start with having the child submerge just their mouth, then move to their whole face.

○ **Family Water Fight!**
Play with water guns, water balloons, or wet sponges.

○ Go **Bobbing for Apples**.
Place apples in a large pot or basin filled with water. Challenge the child to retrieve an apple without using their hands. Experiment with other foods. Bobbing for peapods, anyone?

○ Walk into a pool.
Have the child start in the shallow end and, over subsequent exposures, walk toward the deeper end.

○ Play underwater games.
The child can swim through someone's legs, dive for treasure, or play **Marco Polo**.

○ Visit a water park.

Also: Uncertainty

WEATHER
Considerations

Exposure for weather-related fears is appropriate when the level of fear far exceeds actual danger. If there is a history of trauma associated with a weather event, such as a child's house burned down or someone known to the child was killed by lightning, trauma-informed therapy should be done prior to initiating exposure-based interventions.

Weather fears sometimes center on particular weather events such as tornadoes or floods, and sometimes on aspects of the weather such as wind or clouds. Substitute the child's particular fear in the exposures listed below. The aim of these exposures is to get the child talking about and imagining the feared weather event while reducing safety behaviors. Keep in mind that there are many ways to check the weather including looking outside, asking parents, and checking forecasts.

Exposures

○ Make art out of weather words.
   Have the child write weather words in bubble letters and color them in. Hang the weather terms around the house.

○ Do a **Word Search** with weather words.
   There are websites that will create a Word Search for you from relevant keywords such as: tornado, thunder, hurricane, typhoon, rain, blizzard, or lightning.

○ Look up weather terms and what they mean.

○ Read a fact book about weather.

○ Play **Weather Charades**.

○ Say the weather words out loud.
   Move from having the child say the triggering word once to saying it repeatedly, then adding, "It's possible that a [feared weather event] could happen."

○ Draw a picture of the kind of weather that scares you.

○ Read a story about the kind of weather you don't like.

○ Make up a story about being out in bad weather.

○ Act out being out in bad weather.
   Have the child use dolls, puppets, or small figures to act out being outside during the feared weather.

○ Look at pictures of the weather that scares you.
   The adult should prescreen and adjust for scariness before showing pictures to the child.

○ Listen to weather sounds.
   Have the child listen to sounds associated with the feared weather event a little at a time, then increase the volume and duration. The adult can begin by leaving the weather sounds on in the background at low volume while the child is doing another activity such as coloring or playing checkers, then move to listening in a focused way.

○ Watch videos of the weather.

Watch initially without sound, then with the volume low, and finally at full volume. Move from watching a fictional weather event in a children's movie to live footage, with an adult prescreening for appropriateness beforehand.

○ Make weather sounds.

This can be done with rain sticks or fans, or by drumming on a sheet of metal. Have the child participate in making the sounds, then listen to a recording of them. Move toward listening alone while reading about the target weather event.

How to Make a Rain Stick

1. Find a sturdy cardboard tube. Decorate it.
2. Trace the end of the tube two times onto a grocery bag or construction paper.
3. Draw a second circle, about 1 inch larger, around each of the tube-size circles.
4. Cut out the larger circles.
5. Cut small snips in from the larger circles to the smaller circles to make fringe around the smaller circles.
6. Place one fringed circle at the end of the cardboard tube and attach with tape or rubber bands.
7. Tear several strips of aluminum foil and roll them tightly the long way.
8. Spiral the rolled foil around a pencil. Remove the pencil and drop the spirals into the tube.
9. Collect a half-cup of any combination of uncooked rice, dried beans, or small plastic beads and pour them into the tube. Different sizes, shapes, and materials will produce different sounds.
10. Attach the remaining fringed paper circle to the open end of the tube using tape or rubber bands.
11. Turn end-to-end, and let the rain dance begin!

○ Only check the forecast once.

Kids are resourceful, and may be checking the weather on television, online, or in the newspaper in addition to asking parents about it. A token system can work here, as can setting specific, limited times that checking is allowed. Work toward having the child only check the weather once to choose what to wear that day.

○ Stand under a roof outside when it is rainy or windy.

○ Go out when rain, clouds, or wind is in the forecast.

Move from going out when bad weather is expected to going out in actual bad weather, and from brief to longer excursions.

Also: Intrusive Thoughts, Uncertainty, Words and Phrases

WIPING
Considerations
Anxiety about wiping can go two ways. The first is a refusal to wipe seen in children with an intense fear of inadvertently touching poop. The second is over-wiping, where children panic about the possibility of not being entirely clean.

For children who avoid wiping, the therapist can reframe poop as somewhat yucky, but not dangerous. Coach parents to treat wiping as a routine task, done without disgust or fear. As exposure to wiping gets underway, it is important for parents to acknowledge the child may get poop on their hands, which is easily remedied with normal handwashing.

Children who overwipe are typically intent on achieving absolute cleanliness, seeking reassurance that they are clean, repeatedly checking toilet paper for evidence of stool, and changing clothing when they are done, driven by the fear that it has somehow gotten wet or dirty. The aim of exposure is to help children learn to tolerate the uncertainty they feel as they move away from each of these safety behaviors.

Exposures
OVERWIPING

○ Wipe an appropriate number of times.
Begin by having the child count the number of wipes they typically do, then have them subtract one every few days. The other option, best for children who continue to wipe after the toilet paper is clean, is to reduce and then eliminate extra wipes.

○ Use an appropriate amount of toilet paper.
The parent can start with the child's baseline and reduce over time. Or they can count out a certain number of sheets ahead of time and have the child use that amount, or less. Consider rewarding the child for toilet paper left unused.

○ Wipe a random number of times.
Use a die or decide how many times to wipe by picking a number out of a bag.

○ Wait between using the toilet and changing clothes.
Encourage the child to return to normal activity while waiting to change their clothes. There is no need for a parent to set an alarm or tell the child

when time is up. If the child notices on their own and wants to change, they should be allowed to do so, but by the time they get to 20 minutes, most children find that the urge to change has vanished.

○ Wear one pair of underwear a day.
Some children want to change their underwear repeatedly, worrying they may have gotten it wet or dirty. Start with their baseline number of changes, reducing systematically by one until the child is wearing just one pair per day.

○ Make your underwear wet on purpose.
Have the child dribble a bit of water onto their underwear after using the toilet, then continue to wear it.

WIPING AVOIDANCE

○ Be in charge of the toilet paper.
Have the child remove toilet paper from the roll, prepare it for use, and hand it to the parent for wiping.

○ Play **Find It** in the bathroom.
Have a parent hide a small plastic toy in various spots in the bathroom, beginning with fairly obvious places like peeking out from behind the shower curtain. Over subsequent rounds of the game, choose hiding places that are harder to see or access such as in the linen closet or behind the toilet. The goal in this game, beyond finding the figurine, is for the child to touch cabinets, door knobs, and other parts of the bathroom they might see as germy.

○ Flush the toilet without using your hands.
If the child avoids flushing the toilet, challenge them to find the perfect flusher, an elbow, perhaps, or a sturdy pencil. Make the game harder by having them come up with a unique way to flush each time.

○ Flush the toilet with your hand.
Move from using a square of toilet paper as a barrier to flushing barehanded.

○ Stay in the bathroom after using the toilet and washing hands.
Increase the time the child stays in the bathroom. Build in distractions like telling jokes or playing **I Spy** at the start, then phase these out so the child is more aware of intentionally staying in the bathroom.

○ Wait a minute between pooping and flushing.

○ Look in the toilet after pooping.
  Have the child look at their waste in the toilet. Increase time spent looking, going from quick glances to more sustained examination. Pretend to be poop-ologists by describing the poop in pseudoscientific ways, or act like museum tour guides showcasing an interesting exhibit. Be playful as you find ways to describe the color, texture, and smell of the child's poop, and encourage the child to do the same.

○ Touch the toilet seat.
  Have the child move from quick to sustained touching and from the top of the seat to the underside. Allow handwashing after this exposure.

○ Have a **Thumb Fight** or play a **Clapping Game**.
  Have the parent play a game with the child in the bathroom after wiping and washing.

○ Pretend to wipe while wearing clothes.
  Have the child move from making wiping motions without actually touching their clothes to wiping over just their underwear.

○ Touch your own bottom.
  Have the child touch their own bottom with their hands, first the outer aspects, then the cheeks, and finally the crack where their cheeks come together. Wash hands afterward.

○ Practice wiping your bottom at times other than after pooping.
  This can be done after urinating or at other times not connected to toileting. Move from a single wipe to multiple wipes.

○ Wipe using a disposable glove.
  Move from making a single wipe and having the parent do the rest to fully wiping, all with the glove in place. Progress from having the parent remove the child's glove to having the child do it.

○ Take over wiping mid-way through, without a glove.
  Move from having the child make the final wipe to having the child wipe after a certain number of parental wipes, decreasing the number of parental wipes over time.

○ Do the first wipe without a glove.
  Have the child begin and the parent finish wiping. Gradually increase the number of wipes the child is asked to do.

○ Use fewer wet-wipes.
Eventually get to where wet-wipes are used for the final wipe or not at all.

Also: Contamination, Toileting

WITCHES
See: Baddies

WORDS AND PHRASES
Considerations
Anxious children frequently ban particular words or phrases associated with their fears, and parents often accommodate to avoid meltdowns. Exposure includes slowly removing this accommodation, saying the words and phrases on purpose before moving to the natural exposure inherent in unfiltered speech.

When treating specific phobias, the therapist may need to desensitize the child to relevant words before moving to more formal exposure hierarchies. For example, you might have to desensitize a child to the word *vomit* before progressing through a hierarchy targeting the fear of throwing up. The following exposures can be done with any word or phrase, from common words to curse words, and from mundane-seeming to more disturbing intrusive thoughts.

Exposures

○ Write the word or phrase with your finger.
Have the child "finger-paint" triggering words and phrases without the paint, write the words in sand, or write with water on a piece of paper.

○ Write the word and then quickly get rid of it.
Move from writing the word on a dry-erase board or paper and immediately erasing or destroying it to leaving the word or phrase in place.

○ Make word art.
Have the child make bubble letter posters, decorative placemats, and fancy font renditions of the offending word or phrase. Hang them around the home.

○ Spell the word or phrase with your body.
For example, an "A" can be made with legs spread wide and hands joined

overhead and a "T" by holding arms perpendicular to shoulders. Turn body-spelling into a guessing game.

○ Read the word or phrase silently, then out loud.

○ Play **Remote Control**.
Take turns using a pretend remote control, prompting one another to turn the volume of the triggering words up, up, up, and then down. Use the full range, from silently mouthing the word or phrase at the low end to shouting it at the high end.

○ Say the word or phrase repeatedly.
Challenge the child to say it ten times fast, then twenty times, then thirty. Use a timer to see who can do it fastest.

○ Use apps to play with the word.
Have the child speak the word or phrase into an app that changes tone of voice or turns spoken language into a rap.

○ Sing the word or phrase to the tune of a familiar song.

○ Write a song, limerick, haiku, rap, or poem with the word or phrase.

○ Create an **Acrostic** with the word or phrase. Have the child write the word or phrase vertically on a page, then write related words starting with each of the letters.

> **Word Play with Trigger-Words**
> ✔ Say it ten times fast.
> ✔ Say it in Pig Latin.
> ✔ Say it backward.
> ✔ Say it like a baby.
> ✔ Say it like a cat.
> ✔ Say it in different volumes.
> ✔ Say it s-l-o-w-l-y.
> ✔ Say it while pretending your mouth is full.
> ✔ Say it with your mouth closed.
> ✔ Say it quietly, then get louder and louder.
> ✔ Say it with an accent.
> ✔ Say it with water in your mouth.
> ✔ Sing it to the tune of a familiar song.
> ✔ Say it as though you are sharing good news.
> ✔ Say it while exaggerating the vowels.
> ✔ Say it while making different facial expressions.

○ Say the word or phrase in different voices or accents.

○ Play **Go Fish**.
Write variations of the word or phrase on index cards, putting each word or phrase onto sets of two cards or four. Shuffle and deal the cards. For example, if you were playing Go Fish with weather terms, you would ask one another, "Do you have a hurricane?" "Do you have thunder?" "Do you have a tornado?" Don't get too caught up in whether or not the questions make sense.

○ Write a paragraph that uses the word or phrase repeatedly.
Have the child record themself reading the paragraph. Listen to the recording, aiming for 5 minutes several times a day.

○ Have a silly conversation using only the word or phrase.
Using gestures, tone of voice, and inflection, have a nonsensical conversation about, for example, what to have for dinner, using only the triggering words and phrases.

Also: Intrusive Thoughts, Uncertainty

X-RAYS
See: Dentists, Doctors, Medical Procedures

YACKING

See: Speaking, Vomiting

YELLOWJACKETS

See: Bees

YES
Considerations

Some children approach the world apprehensively and have a hard time saying "Yes" to new experiences. This fear is addressed elsewhere.

See: Change in Plans, Mistakes, Perfectionism, Trying New Things

ZOMBIES
See: Baddies

About the Authors

Dr. Dawn Huebner is a Psychologist, Parent Coach, and the author of numerous self-help books for children including bestsellers *What to Do When You Worry Too Much* and *Outsmarting Worry*. Specializing in childhood anxiety, Dr. Huebner's work is known around the world, with books translated into 23 languages. She has been featured on "The Today Show," WebMD, *Parents Magazine*, and a host of other news and information outlets. The parent of a once-anxious child, Dr. Huebner faced anxiety in her own life, making the same mistakes most parents make before finding the keys to breaking herself and her child free. She now teaches those keys to others, sharing with parents, therapists, school counselors, and educators the skills they need to help anxious children live happier lives. Her TEDx talk, *Rethinking Anxiety*, has been viewed over a million times.

Dr. Erin Neely is a Clinical Psychologist who has worked for the past 20 years to make the lives of children and their families happier and easier. Dr. Neely grew up in the Washington DC area, did her undergraduate training in theater at Syracuse University, and obtained her doctorate in clinical psychology from Widener University. While being trained as a generalist, Dr. Neely came to recognize her passion for working with children, particularly children on the autism spectrum. These remarkable children and families taught her about the medical complexities of ASD, leading her to become a certified integrative nutrition coach. She combined her creative heart and her clinical knowledge to make her YouTube channel, Miss Erin Doctor, where she educates children on mental health topics such as ERP through fun, easy-to-understand animations. When children ask Dr. Neely what she does for work, she happily tells them, "This!" meaning playing with them. Universally, they will say something like, "Lucky." And she agrees.